LOBBYCRATIC GOVERNANCE

DEDICATION

This book is dedicated to Sergey Diakanov, a very talented artist, architect and writer who developed the cover of this book.

He guided the trip that my wife and I took to the former Soviet Union in 1993. He subsequently designed dozens of book covers, posters and logos for our various clients and projects while he was also designing and supervising the construction of a number of industrial buildings in Russia.

Sergey went missing from his Moscow apartment in June 2016. The reason for his sudden and mysterious disappearance may never be resolved despite the best efforts of the police, his family and friends to locate him.

Sergey's talent will live long into the future in the art he has left behind and the ideas he shared with all who knew him.

Godfrey Harris
July 2016

LOBBYCRATIC GOVERNANCE

HOW TO LIMIT THE POWER TECHNOCRATS AND LOBBYISTS WIELD OVER OUR LIVES

GODFREY HARRIS

THE AMERICAS GROUP
520 S. Sepulveda Blvd., Suite 204
Los Angeles, CA 90049 USA

The Americas Group
520 S. Sepulveda Blvd., Suite 204
Los Angeles, California 90049-3534
U.S.A.

☎   + (1) 310 476 6374
FX   + (1) 310 471 3276
EM   hrmg@mac.com
WWW   AMERICASGROUP.COM

ISBN:
978-0-935047-86-8

Library of Congress Cataloging-in-Publication Data

Names: Harris, Godfrey, 1937- author.
Title: Lobbycratic governance : how to limit the power technocrats and lobbyists / Godfrey Harris.
Description: Los Angeles, California : Americas Group, 2016. | Includes   bibliographical references and index.
1Identifiers: LCCN 2016029243 | ISBN 9780935047868
Subjects: LCSH: Lobbying--United States. | Pressure groups--United States. | Political culture--United States. | United States--Politics and government.
Classification: LCC JK1118 .H365 2016 | DDC 324/.40973--dc23
LC record available at https://lccn.loc.gov/2016029243

Printed in India by
AEGEAN OFFSET PRINTING, LTD.

TABLE OF CONTENTS

ABOUT THE AUTHOR

 **GODFREY HARRIS** has been a public policy consultant based in Los Angeles, California, since 1968. He began consulting on government affairs after teaching American and comparative government at UCLA and Rutgers; serving as an intelligence officer on a U.S. Army post in the Northeast; a U.S. foreign service officer in Bonn, London, and Washington; an organizational specialist in President Lyndon Johnson's Executive Office and as a project manager for an international financial company in Geneva.

In all of these positions, Harris studied the people and programs of government to understand how they work, where they are vulnerable, and how they can be changed. He has applied his knowledge to countless projects for such clients as the Departments of State, Commerce, and Housing and Urban Development as well as the London Chamber of Commerce and the Foreign Policy Association of Panama.

Harris has focused on politics his entire career. As President of Harris/Ragan Management Group, he has focused the firm's activities on projects that offer alternative solutions to matters of community concern. As such, he has served as a registered foreign agent, as a lobbyist for various interest groups, as the manager of several election campaigns, and as an advisor to private companies dealing with government at all levels.

Harris has written 75 other books on his own or with associates. He holds degrees from Stanford University and the University of California, Los Angeles.

A STRATEGY FOR READING
LOBBYCRATIC GOVERNANCE

The drive to know everything that happens as it happens seems all-consuming in America today. What we absorb from moment to moment is coming at us in multiple ways:

- *Personal observations*
- *Conversations*
- *Phone calls*
- *Emails*
- *Text messages*
- *Tweets*
- *Facebook notes*
- *Instagram postings*
- *Alerts from major news outlets*
- *News flashes on 24/7 television channels.*

As a result, a book that argues a point of view on a governmental topic may give the impression of being better suited to a political science seminar than to the kind of discussion on politics common today.

I hope, however, that the initial reaction to a book about the interconnection among lobbyists, technocrats, politicians and lawyers is not one of wariness but rather one of curiosity about what changes may be needed and are possible in the way America is actually governed.

If potential readers are intrigued enough to delve further into the book in some depth, here is a strategy to get the most out of whatever time can be devoted to it:

- *Review the first chapter "Lobbycratic Governance in Brief." It makes the headline point that the U.S. government no longer resembles the fairy tale taught in high school civics classes or the government that your father dealt with.*

- *Review one or more of the individual chapters that discuss how lobbyists and their technocratic colleagues ascended to power, aided by lawyers and enabled by elected and appointed officials, with the citizenry pushed back to observer status. Each of the chapters provides anecdotes, statistics and examples to support the basic premise that a government taken from the people can still be recovered by the people.*

- *The book concludes with a number of suggestions for changing the current dynamics to get government closer to Lincoln's ideal of one that is of, by and for the people.*

This is a book based on anecdotes, impressions and observations, but short of hard "evidence" for every opinion, strong "proof" for every assertion or a conclusive "basis" for every suggestion. America's penchant to justify everything with "fact" may come from our legalistic culture. The truth, however, is that politics is mostly about perceptions and that an informed impression can be as accurate and as controlling on how people deal with government in a modern society as any indisputable fact or election result.

Godfrey Harris
Los Angeles

July 2016

1.
LOBBYCRATIC GOVERNANCE IN BRIEF

Abraham Lincoln famously described the essence of American government as —

of the people, by the people, for the people.

Unfortunately, the government of the United States does not come close to fulfilling that description.

The American people have allowed their national government to change and evolve in ways that now makes Lincoln's dictum a fantasy.

In reality —

> **America's federal government has become a centralized group of managerial and regulatory agencies run by technocrats working on their own or with lobbyists representing large special interest groups, whose efforts are refined by legal specialists and facilitated by both elected and appointed officials.**

This single sentence succinctly describes how the American citizenry has allowed itself to be frozen out of what I call —

lobbycratic governance.

A system controlled by technocrats, advised by lobbyists, operated in conjunction with their lawyers, and facilitated by politicians is not the government most think is running the United States. Elected and appointed officials have become subservient to a vast army of civil servants.

How else do you explain the fact that the Secretary of State can be charged in 2016 by the Department's Inspector General with a dereliction of responsibility for not having sought the permission of civil servants to use a private email system to communicate her ideas and thoughts. The IG said that had she asked "it would not have been granted." It was, he said, contrary to "Departmental policy." No one questioned how the Secretary of State, an officer selected by the President and vetted by the Senate to be in charge of departmental policy, could nevertheless be subservient to the dictates of career government employees. Later, the Attorney General said she would abide by the decisions of professional prosecutors to determine if any charges would be filed against Mrs. Clinton. None were. It was another clear example of how politicians have surrendered control of the government of the United States to the technocrats in Washington.

Who is to blame (or credit) for this and many other changes in politics over the last 50 years? Politico's co-founder expressed it this way in early 2016: "… establishment America has grown fat, lazy, conventional and deserving of radical disruption." Moreover, at the beginning of the 20th century, citizens didn't need government permission to go fishing, collect rain water, use a vehicle, renovate a home, own a weapon or enter a profession. Now official approval to engage in any of these activities or others is required. How we got into this situation and how we get out of it is the essence of this book.

The national pattern of lobbycratic governance is replicated in international organizations, the big states and most of the major cities. Take the State of New York and its Department of Corrections and Community Supervision. It is a government agency effectively owned and operated by lobbyists for the Correctional Officers & Police Benevolent Association. In the words of *The New York Times*, the organization's 20,000 members have "long held the levers of power inside [New York's] prisons."[†]

The union is a formidable force in New York electoral politics as well. It exerts its influence over legislators in districts where prisons are the biggest employer. For example, the chairman of the corrections committee of the State Senate has no fewer than five prison facilities in his district. The governor's chief of staff previously worked in public relations for the prison union, and her father is a union lobbyist who earned nearly $700,000 between 2010 and 2015 on union business. The *Times* says that this union is so powerful that one guard found guilty of brutalizing an inmate still could not be fired from his job.

[†]This union is apparently is no slouch at corruption. Its president was arrested in June 2016 because of a cash award he received for directing a $20 million investment of the union's money to a high-risk hedge fund that other investors were abandoning.

Most people are outraged when they hear these kinds of stories about blatant abuse of police authority and shake their heads when they learn how raw union power is used to preserve jobs no matter the circumstances. It isn't ideological. These same people are stunned when they hear of welfare excesses, the enormous pensions paid to civil servants, or the opposition to any laws of any kind that restrict unfettered access to guns.

The problem is that these same people do not see themselves as complicit in the situations that have slowly corrupted our system of government. They do not equate their responsibilities as citizens with any of the problems they see around them. On the contrary, they have their own little cheats from shaving income on tax forms, taking personal deductions as business expenses, accepting special discounts, inflating resumes, scalping tickets, rolling through stop signs, using office supplies for school projects, and on and on. It may well be why they silently accept, even if they don't always condone, the negative activities occurring in the public sector.

One of the reasons for the abdication of American governance is the boredom that most experienced in high school civics classes. Peggy Noonan attributes some of it to an "epochal end of public faith in institutions." Lobbyists for large organizations working with high level technocrats in executive agencies, guided by legal staffs to keep their decisions within boundaries established by the judicial system, have filled the vacuum left by the people's negligence. Most citizens, it seems, don't care and probably won't wake up to the threat to their control, despite constant media articles on political scandal and corruption, Internet videos on how the system is manipulated, and books like these. When citizens finally *do* start paying attention, it may be too late to do anything to return the country to the path that provides a government of, by and for the people.

Some would say that Americans are getting what they deserve. The shame is that their indifference is taking the rest of us who *do* care with them. Why are a majority of Americans ignoring the government abuses they hear about and sometimes experience? They say they are too busy with job and family; they say they have more important things to do with hobbies and recreational pursuits; they say their time is taken by volunteer work for their church, local school or a needy charity.

But none of these reasons overrides the responsibility of citizens to play a role in the government of a democracy. Whether a person doesn't vote, cheats on taxes, lies about his or her availability to serve on a jury, knowingly defies traffic laws, or consistently ignores the norms of society for his or her own benefit, his behavior leaves the doors of government open for others to walk through and pick the pockets of those least able to protect themselves. All of this can be fixed and this book hopes to show how it can be done — if citizens are willing to put in the effort to effect real change. If they aren't, matters will only get worse.

The methodical accumulation of power by lobbyists employed by politically and economically powerful organizations working in association with government technocrats began with the formation of the Interstate Commerce Commission in 1887. It is a pattern that was accepted during the Roosevelt and Wilson eras, found permanence during the New Deal, and effectively took control of the entire United States government in the Johnson Administration.

Despite this reality and evidence that abounds, Americans still cling to a myth about how the American government works. For example, citizens are constantly urged by political leaders, major foundations and media voices to participate in the solution to the country's problems. Get involved! But few suggestions by those outside of the mix of technocrats, lobbyists, organization leaders, politicians and media representatives — America's governing elite — ever actually get considered or implemented. Why? It is hard for those paid to solve problems to accept solutions from those who are not part of their magic insider circle.

The same governing elite is also continually harping on the need for citizens to vote during every election. These pleas are as much a ritual of American governance as fireworks on the 4th of July. But *voting* as a means of determining the direction of the United States is now close to a fraud, given the way election procedures tend to be successfully manipulated to a consensus conclusion — in most cases by a consortium of monied interests, media desires and professional political operatives.

As the noted anarchist Emma Goldman said: "If voting changed anything, they'd make it illegal."

Because of this reality, only about half of the eligible population bothers to cast ballots on a regular basis for President and many fewer than that in non-presidential years and for lesser offices.

Maybe those who don't consistently vote are really too busy taking care of jobs and family; perhaps they really do get confused by all the conflicting rhetoric they hear in the campaigns leading up to an election. But clearly many don't think their participation in an election makes much difference in how the government is run or how it affects their lives. They have concluded that —

Voting doesn't much matter in the way government really works in the United States today.

In fact, voting in America has become a bit like kabuki theater in Japan. The performers move, dialog is spoken and the dances unfold — but the stylized structure of the show remains constant and the outcome is pre-ordained. So, too, with American elections. As Senator David Perdue of Georgia put it: "In the Senate . . . this drive to get reelected trumps everything else in Washington."

The candidates and their supporters spend enormous amounts of money; campaigns publish important sounding issue papers that no one other than the opposition actually reads; newspapers, mail channels, airwaves and blogs are flooded with election chatter and brutally negative comments; and the candidates ricochet around their electoral districts making speeches, attending rallies and seeking even more money to do more of whatever they have been doing to ensure an election victory.

But the modern reality is that few office holders running for reelection *lose*. In 2014, for example, 96.4 percent of Congressional incumbents were re-elected despite an approval rating of 11 to 14 percent! How can this be? Gerrymandered districts is one reason, name recognition and constituent services is another. Policy positions? Hardly.

Then when the votes are counted and political pundits pontificate on the portents of what has just taken place, nothing really changes: The country returns to its daily concerns and those with a stake in managing lobbycratic governance return to their roles of adjusting the levers of power to meet the special needs and interests of their patrons and particular constituencies.

The reality is that elections in the U.S. don't change the machinery of governance very much. Oh, yes, one or two new personalities emerge, a few fresh rags-to-riches stories come to light, and a different count of membership in this group or that faction is identified. But the management system that has been developed and refined by the technocrats, lobbyists, lawyers and politicians for the past 50 years remains essentially the same election after election.

Barack Obama is the only President in this or the last century to be *re-elected* by fewer votes than he received in his first Presidential campaign. Who knew that between 2008 and 2014, more voters in more districts were trending conservative than progressive? As a result, Democrats lost 13 Senate seats, 69 House seats, 10 governorships and 917 seats in state legislatures. Did it matter? Not a whit.

But this indifference may have started to change in 2015. The level of dissatisfaction in the country with the old patterns and accepted traditional ways was palpable. Just look at some of the rhetoric and polling numbers spilling out across the media trying to explain Donald Trump's ascendancy and Bernie Sanders's appeal as well as the problems that Jeb Bush, Mario Rubio, Hillary Clinton and other "establishment" candidates experienced during the 2016 election cycle.

Gideon Kanner, a Loyola law school professor writing in the *Los Angeles Daily Journal* in early 2016, says that after years of listening to politicians make claims about new taxes (George H. W. Bush's "read my lips") and the benign changes envisioned for Obamacare (Barack Obama's "you can keep your doctor"), people are angered to the point that they no longer listen to any political babble.

Kanner further explains that people are fed up with a situation where government leaders could be spending the country into insolvency and Social Security could run out of money, yet big banks get interest free loans from the government while still charging credit card holders double digit rates. A good part of this economic activity is funded by borrowing enormous sums from foreign governments while a number of large corporations can evade some or all of their U.S. taxes through a tax code — "so complex and so convoluted" — that not even the IRS can understand and interpret it consistently.[†]

Sometimes the code doesn't have to be manipulated so much as common sense applied. For example, the U.S. marginal corporate tax rate is 39.2 percent — 35 percent at the federal level and 4.2 percent for state taxes, according to figures compiled by the Organization for Economic Cooperation and Development. It reports that the global average is 25 percent.

The Republic of Ireland charges corporations at a rate of 11 percent! Why wouldn't firms look to save shareholders an enormous amount of money by seeking arrangements that would allow them to relocate their headquarters to Ireland? The point is that a growing number of Americans wonder why politicians complain loudly about corporations avoiding their "fair share" to pursue "inversion" tactics, but do *nothing* themselves to try to reform the U.S. tax code to resolve the problems.

Why the reluctance to solve something they have the power and responsibility to fix? Is it a case of laziness or reluctance? Probably more the latter. Once the tax code has been opened to correct one problem, game on to "fix" others. The end result , so the fear goes, might be worse than what we have

---

[†]Listen to what Intuit, the giant developer of financial and tax preparation software (Quicken Books and TurboTax) had to say in a 2016 tax-day full-page ad in *The New York Times*: ". . . our tax code is mind-numbingly complex. [T]here are now 11 different kinds of IRAs, 3 different ways to help with childcare and 14 different education incentives — all with complex rules, various parts phasing in and out, and with widely differing and conflicting definitions of terms, even for something as basic as the meaning of 'dependent.'"

today. But what does that say about the power of politicians versus the lobbyists and technocrats?

Professor Kanner goes on to note that the Supreme Court justices — "openly chosen for their partisan ideology" — at times have preempted democratic processes. He points to the constitutional mandate that limits "the taking of private property to public use" and then reviews decisions that sanction the transfer of middle class property to wealthier individuals for the private gain of the latter. He says that "the *Kelo* case has had an astonishing and unanticipated impact on Americans' understanding of how their government really operates — none of it for the good."

All of the pain captured in this brief summary is also reflected in some poll numbers:

68% of the American people now say they are dissatisfied with the direction of the United States. Only —

8% of the American people rate the honesty and ethics of the Members of Congress as "high." Sadly, just —

34% say they are satisfied with how the American system of government works.

This book explains how we have reached this distressing present position and offers some solutions to get us back to where we were before our fellow citizens decided to leave government to others.

America's government of technocrats working under their own recognizance or with lobbyists, funded by large organizations,

yields major benefits for them. Elected and appointed officials provide legitimacy while lawyers keep the system reasonably balanced between competing interests.

The U.S. federal government is not alone in this pattern of governance. The same forces are working in state capitals and around city halls. In San Diego, a city councilman lamented that a technocrat had installed big jagged rocks to prevent homeless encampments in certain areas. That pushed the homeless deeper into the councilman's district. Rather than use his legislative position to find a workable solution, he "demanded an apology from the city" — as if he were not a part of its government.

Technocrats are also driving policy at the big international organizations. Look at what happens in Brussels. Lobbyists and lawyers hover around the Eurocrats — the European Union's special version of a technocrat — in the development of new policy. The 731 elected members of the EU Parliament are more than four hours away in Strasbourg. Excessive technocratic control of day-to-day life in the interest of equality across the 28 countries, as well as open border policies, were key parts of the Brexit debate in Britain. In June 2016, British voters decided to end the country's participation in the EU.

American government is no longer the government of our fathers where the executive, legislative and judicial branches comprised a system of checks and balances to engender compromise. The new order of American governance looks more like this:

Major corporations, large interest groups,

big labor unions, and other dominant institutions — working with a maze of foundations, think tanks, research firms, academic facilities, and consulting groups — compete to set the country's agenda. Once these competing organizations sort out their differences (green energy advocates, for instance, overpower the Audobon Society and other groups to get the U.S. Fish and Wildlife Service to approve wind turbines that will kill an estimated 4,200 bald eagles a year), their lobbyists join forces with technocrats and lawyers to create an ever-expanding body of implementing regulations with only a few new laws that are reported to the people by a shrinking traditional media sector and a self-serving river of websites.

The defiance of the old ways of implementing policy changes can be clearly seen in a 2016 controversy over transgender bathroom use. In the face of a number of states mandating different policies for their schools on this issue, the Department of Education suddenly declared all schools receiving federal money — that's nearly all 100,000 of them — had to allow students to use facilities relating to their gender identity rather than their sex at birth. The Attorney General of Oklahoma ,writing in *The Wall Street Journal,* noted that the Obama administration had not only illegally changed the definition of "sex" in Title IX of the 1972 Education Act but had made the changes unilaterally without any public comment. It will be for the courts to determine if this aspect of lobbycratic governance will stand.

Average citizens are excluded from participating in these tasks. Since 2008, some of them have become angry enough to want major changes. The rise of the Tea Party on the right and progressive voices on the left are confronting the traditional forces of the political establishment. It reflects a fundamental struggle for control of the direction and management of the government of the United States that is now underway as the political class clings to proximity to power rather than any particular principle of governance.

Contesting elections is just one avenue citizens can travel to regain control of their government. The Internet and social media have proven effective in organizing and fomenting change. Civil disobedience — from the occupation of Malheur National Wildlife Refuge in Oregon to the Black Lives Matter and Occupy Wall Street movements — has become more aggressive and brought added recognition to the discontent brewing.

Much can be done to change the dynamic of lobbycratic governance and to help people regain control of the mechanisms of power. It will not happen, however, if people merely shake their heads, cluck their tongues and complain to friends.

2.
NOT YOUR FATHER'S GOVERNMENT

This book came to be written as a result of the Budget Act of Fiscal Year 2014. The approval of a $3.6 trillion spending plan in December 2013 came at a time when I was simultaneously involved in two projects with public policy implications.

- One dealt with changes in the U.S. rules governing the trade and movement of objects made from or with *ivory;*

- The other involved the random and dysfunctional way Americans tend to give their money to medical, educational, cultural and social service *charities.*

To ease some of the pressure in dealing with both issues for different clients, I went looking for commonalities in the two areas that might save me some time.

I soon realized that public involvement in these two seemingly disparate topics has a lot to do with an understanding of how to the U.S. government *actually* functions in the 21st century. Knowing whom to speak to and how to pitch each issue shortcut the process considerably. That soon led me to the conclusion that government works today in a much different manner from the way I explained it years ago to classes I taught in American and comparative government at UCLA and Rutgers.

To understand those changes, we need to look at how American government was first envisioned. It encompasses the words and images that most of us heard in the 11th grade or learned about in citizenship classes — or still read from time to time in the press.

Having suffered from a tyranny of a far-away government, Americans declared their independence from England in 1776, then fought a war against British troops to defend their new status.[†]

[†]One of the fascinating aspects of this era in American history involves how the War of Independence was fought. Teachers never tell their students that the outcome of the war may have been in large measure because it was fought against second tier British forces — for the most part newly enlisted and experienced soldiers. The best of the British military were deployed to India

Once the more determined Americans had triumphed in the Revolutionary War, they created a decentralized government for their newly independent states. The Confederation was designed to serve as a central government to oversee the common good of the entities sharing the Eastern seaboard from New Hampshire to Georgia. It was a failure.

- The idea of a confederation of 13 equal states reflected the fear that most Americans of the time had of the power that centralized governments could wield. After all, Britain had a centralized government and look how it dealt with its colonies. For the most part the confederation didn't turn out to work any better for the common good than the British colonial model.

- As a result, leaders of the 13 states gathered together in September 1787 to find a way to guide and control a central government with defined, but specifically limited, powers. The U.S. Constitution is the result of how they decided to accomplish that.

---

were deployed to India to protect what King George III knew was an economically more important territory of the Empire. As evidence of the lesser nature of the American colonies in British eyes, note that immediately after George Washington defeated Lord Cornwallis at Yorktown in 1781, King George III thought it such an unimportant aberration that he rewarded the earl with the second most important position in the British Empire. Cornwallis left Yorktown to become Viceroy of India.

The Constitution firmly establishes who is in charge of this new government and what that government is to do. It used these famous words to lock down the point:

> *We the People of the United States, in Order to form a more perfect Union, establish Justice, insure domestic Tranquility, provide for the common defence, promote the general Welfare, and secure the Blessings of Liberty to ourselves and our Posterity, do ordain and establish this Constitution for the United States of America.*

The goals articulated clearly give the new central authority the power to do in a collective way what an individual state could not do as effectively for itself.

PRINCIPAL CHECKS AND BALANCES

But having fought a war against a king that was thought of as tyrannically oppressive — and knowing that too much power has a tendency to corrupt even the best of men with the best of original intentions — the authors of the Constitution devised a bedrock principle of American governance and incorporated it into the basic document they crafted:

> **They *divided* the responsibility of government among three distinct elements, each with different powers — legislative, executive and judicial. The three elements were not co-equal, as is often mistakenly asserted, but they were very well balanced in how they could and could not function.**

The Founding Fathers consciously gave up *efficiency* in the interest of avoiding the dominance of any single force or group.

- The specific powers exercised by what we have come to refer to as the legislative, executive and judicial *branches* of government are enshrined in, or interpreted from, the Constitution. They provide a cleverly nuanced series of *checks* on the power of any one or two of these branches over the remaining branch or branches to ensure a reasonable *balance* among them.[†]

- The checks and balances within the Constitution were crafted not only to curb any excesses that one *branch* might exercise over another but to govern the activities of the two houses of Congress as well. After all, in a reflection on the powers of the monarchy in England, the legislature of the United States was created as the preeminent instrument

---

[†]As an aside, the press has long referred to itself as the "fourth" branch of government because it has assumed the role of watchdog of the three actual branches. The Watergate revelations of the *Washington Post* and the exposure of sexual abuse and cover-ups within the Catholic Church by the *Boston Globe* are just two examples of how effectively that review function has been performed by the nation's press. But, of late, the financial fortunes of most major newspapers has shriveled in the face of the Internet to the point that newspapers are having trouble devoting the resources it takes to maintain the vigilance expected of an effective monitor of major societal institutions. The television networks, more entertainment than enlightenment, have never devoted the resources needed to take on the watchdog role the press has played in the past.

of government. It commands top billing in Article 1 of the Constitution, even if today we think it of secondary importance to the Presidency; an encompassing executive branch did not begin to assert itself until the administration of Teddy Roosevelt.

- Recall, too, that the Senate was conceived in part to perform some of the responsibilities of the British House of Lords — a body of aristocrats that shares executive functions with the monarch.[†] Hence the Senate provides the President with its "advice and consent" for major executive appointees.The Senate was also given a legislative role to be exercised as a body of territorial equals — two senators per state no matter its geographical size, demographic status or economic importance. As such, senators were originally nominated by governors and elected by each state legislature for six-year terms.

- The people were not *directly* involved in the election of senators until the passage of the 17th amendment in 1913. The people are still not *directly* involved in the election of

---

[†]One of the first debates in the first Senate was whether its executive power extended to involvement in the *dismissal* of officers of the government whose appointments it had previously approved. Since many of those who were involved in the writing of the Constitution were elected to the first Congress, they decided that advice and consent meant approval of a nominee's general suitability for office, not a judgment on the person's activities fulfilling the responsibilities of that office. They eventually decided that it was not something they should be involved in.

the President. The Electoral College was invented as a buffer between the people and the selection of a President — another little-recognized element the checks and balances system built into the Constitution.

Much to the consternation of many activitists, when citizens vote for a candidate for the Presidency they are in reality casting ballots for a slate of individual *electors* in their states. Those electors are apportioned — one for each member of the House of Representatives plus two senators — and may or may not be bound by state law to follow the dictates of the popular vote

It is the *electors* pledged to each presidential candidate who are selected on the first Monday after the first Tuesday in November every four years. These electors then assemble in each state capital to formally cast their ballots with the result forwarded to the clerk of the House of Representatives who opens and tallies the *electoral* votes for each candidate before a joint session of Congress. So please note this considerable barrier erected by the Founding Fathers on a government of, by and for the *people*. The barrier still exists and still plays a significant role in presidential politics.

- If the Senate were to be a legislative body with executive powers removed from the direct influence of the people, then the House of Representatives was to be a legislative body *of* the people. As such its members are directly elected by the people for two-year terms to keep them closer to the will of the citizenry and apportioned on the basis of population — with the larger states having more representatives than the smaller ones. Here the "check and balance" idea was to prevent the emotional tides of the "mob" (in theory, the people represented in the House) from overwhelming the sober judgement of a Senate elected *in camera* for a longer term of office and far from the influences of their ragtag neighbors.

But to be sure that the U.S. *legislature* itself would not gain dictatorial dominance of the government — such as Parliaments had achieved from time to time in England — the checks and balances affecting the *houses* of Congress go much further than a mere separation between House and Senate. For instance:

+ Any bill proposed and approved by one house of the Congress must be identical in form and substance to the bill passed by the other house in order to be sent to the President for potential approval.

+ Once both houses agree on the same new piece of legislation, it must be accepted by the President to have the force of law — a check by the executive branch on the potential excesses of the legislative branch.

+ Should the President refuse to sign a Congressional bill into law because he disagrees with it — referred to as the veto power (*veto* in Latin is "I forbid") — the President's rejection *checks* the legislative power but does not end it. The legislature can eradicate the presidential rejection if two-thirds of the members of each house vote to approve the law a second time. They can also decide to pass an altered bill to meet the President's objections or scuttle the original bill in its entirety.

+ Any statute thought to be contrary to the tenets of the nation's basic law may be challenged within the judicial system. While not expressly provided by the drafters of the Constitution, the Supreme Court decided early on that any question of the constitutionality of a law would be the ultimate responsibility of the judiciary. Chief Justice John Marshall reasoned that logic, if nothing else, demanded that the Supreme Court exercise this role. The power was explained by the Supreme Court in its famous *Marbury v. Madison* decision in 1803.[†]

[†]The background that led to that momentous decision is worth reviewing: President John Adams signed the commissions of Federalists he had appointed to new judicial offices on the last day of his term. The commissions were sealed by John Marshall in his capacity as acting Secretary of State, thus authenticating the validity of the signature and the document. But in the days before electronic facilities were available, the signed and sealed commissions could not be delivered to the office holders on that day. The Republicans took control of the Federal government the next day. Newly inaugurated President Thomas Jefferson, fearing the havoc a packed Federalist judiciary might do to laws

Whenever the Supreme Court's power is exercised, the checks and balances come back into play. The losing side in a Supreme Court case has the right to try to correct whatever flaws were found in a piece of legislation or can try to amend the Constitution itself to permit the prohibited activity to flourish. That's exactly what happened in the famous 1920 case of *Missouri v. Holland,* a case that established the

fhis party were intent on enacting, said the appointments were invalid because the commissions had not been delivered to their recipients during President Adams's term. William Marbury was to be a Justice of the Peace for the District of Columbia.

He sued Jefferson's new Secretary of State, James Madison, to compel him to provide the proof of office to which he had lawfully been appointed, approved and felt entitled. The Supreme Court essentially finessed the issue of entitlement while setting a much more important precedent.

John Marshall, having been elevated to the position of Chief Justice, held that Mr. Marbury was indeed entitled to his commission, but the Court could not *compel* its delivery by the Jefferson Administration because the Judiciary Act, which had given Mr. Marbury the right to bring his petition *directly* to the Supreme Court, was flawed.

That Act accorded the Supreme Court new powers of original jurisdiction that were *not* included in the specific powers enumerated for the Court in the Constitution. The law, the court said, could not be enforced.

Ever since *Marbury*, the Supreme Court has been accepted as the unquestioned final stop for appeals from lesser court decisions and the final determinant of what is and what is not valid under the Constitution.

Federal government's primacy in foreign affairs.

A Supreme Court ruling had held that laws involving migratory birds went beyond the interstate commerce clause of the Constitution. So Congress empowered the State Department to negotiate a treaty with the United Kingdom (then in charge of Canada's foreign relations). The Migratory Bird Treaty Act of 1918 was subsequently ratified and came into force. It required the federal government to enact rules to regulate the capture, killing or sale of protected migratory birds. The state of Missouri sued the federal government on the basis that it had no authority to negotiate a treaty on this topic. In holding the act that implemented the treaty constitutional, Justice Oliver Wendell Holmes specifically noted that a *treaty* outweighs any consideration of states' rights or the Tenth Amendment.

The status of the Court as the last stop for deciding the most contentious issues of government[†] has been replicated by many other nations and is considered to be America's greatest contribution to the functioning of a democracy.

[†]Recall that the Court settled the 2000 Presidential election with a 5 to 4 decision in *Bush v. Gore* with nary a peep of protest from the losing side. The verdict gave the election to George W. Bush. The population accepted the result and the country moved on. Indeed, when President Bush entered office a month later he had a 64 percent approval rating.

While the major checks and balances are well known, there are a number of equally effective but lesser known elements that should be noted.

- Congress must generate the funds and then determine how they are to be spent by the Executive branch. While Presidents used to be able to refuse to *spend* funds considered to be excessive or inappropriate, a 1973 law requires Congressional approval to impound funds. The power to *delay* spending money , however, remains yet another of the ways the U.S. constitutional system works to balance the powers of the branches.

- The President is prevented from cronyism by a provision of the Constitution that demands that his appointees to executive and judicial branch positions be approved by two-thirds of the Senate. He has, however, unlimited power to make executive branch appointments and have those appointees fulfill the duties of their office when the Congress is in recess. An absent Congress, particularly in the days of slower travel and no air conditioning, was deemed insufficient reason to cripple the functions of government. Yet, a single senator can now object to consideration of a nominee for an executive branch position and need not engage in a filibuster strategy to have his position prevail. It has happened continuously in the last several years. It effectively prevents the Senate from providing its advice and consent to the President and as a result limits his ability to execute the laws.

- The President's overwhelming authority to conduct the foreign policy of the United States is nevertheless checked by another constitutional provision that requires the Senate to approve all treaties by a two-thirds vote. But a little recognized check in the foreign policy realm also devolves on the House of Representatives. If a treaty involves expenditures of any kind to enforce or implement its provisions, the House of Representatives must initiate an appropriation. The monetary role of the House balances the President's lead position on foreign policy and the advice and consent power of the Senate.

- While the President and the legislature determine what is or is not against the law and punishable, the judicial branch interprets these laws. But in an ancient right borrowed from the rule of kings, the power to *pardon* — to forgive someone for a violation of law — still rests exclusively with the President of the United States. Article II, Section 2, Clause 1 of the Constitution reads:

"The President . . . shall have Power to grant Reprieves and Pardons for Offences against the United States, except in Cases of Impeachment.

Even though he can't pardon himself, this power is nevertheless an important part of ensuring a fair, just and compassionate government. Interestingly, President Obama has used his pardon power more than his six predecessors *combined* and apparently intends to keep using it until his second term expires. Mr. Obama feels obligated to free federal prisoners for what he calls "unjust" sentences associated with low level drug offenses.

- He might free more such prisoners except for a sluggish bureaucracy — yet another little recognized, but significant, element of the checks and balances system. The pardon review process involves seven steps, including asking the original prosecuting attorney for his views on clemency for someone he or she had worked hard to send to prison. Too often, observers have noted, those attorneys have viewed clemency as a rebuke for having accomplished a goal. Delays and objections rendered by career government officials are just another example of a check on executive power and a powerful tool of technocrats in lobbycratic governance. Harry Truman famously articulated this check on presidential power after Dwight Eisenhower's election. He told aides something to the effect that "Ike will bang his fist on the desk, demand that something happen and it won't. In the Army, they jumped. Here they'll shrug, and there won't be a thing he can do about it."

The purpose of these various checks and balances is to ensure that no element of the government goes too far in changing the fundamental compact between the central authority and the powers originally conferred on it by the people. While impressive in imagination and construction, the checks and balances do not work as effectively as in the past.

For one thing, they have been crippled by a refusal of one or another branch to cooperate with another branch. For example:

- President Nixon decided not to spend money for certain government functions desired by a majority in Congress. The power to impound was long a presidential prerogative until an affronted Congress changed the law in 1973.

- The Republican majority in the Senate determined not to consider President Barack Obama's nomination of Merrick Garland to replace Justice Antonin Scalia, claiming that the choice of a new justice should be left to a new President after his or her inauguration in 2017. No hearings were held.

- President Obama has taken several steps to work around what his administration considers Congressional intransigence — including on immigration reform and gun control. In a startling defiance of the original concept of separation of powers, he has issued executive orders under existing but, in some cases, questionable statutory authority and legal precedents. His rationale is that if policies desired by the American people are not likely to be enshrined in new legislation, he will see to getting the job done himself.

One example of this reflects not only on the issue of separation of powers but on the nature of lobbycratic governance itself. It concerns the matter of equal pay for equal work. Feminist organizations have long sought to get the Paycheck Fairness Act approved to serve women who, they argue, are paid less than men for comparable work. Because the act has languished in Congress since 1997 — and has no chance of passage in a Republican-controlled legislature — the Obama administration decided to do one of its "work-arounds." The Obama appointees to the Equal Employment Opportunity Commission have issued new regulations under the Paperwork Reduction Act of 1980 to help determine payroll discrimination.

Critics complain that rather than *reduce* paperwork to comply with government demands, the new regulations *increase* the reporting burden on larger firms to provide wage data "in 14 different gender/race/ethnicity groups, within 12 pay bands and 10 occupational categories." Specifically they note that the EEOC form used for basic wage information will balloon from 140 data points to 3,360 data points. Worse still, branch offices with more than 50 employees would also have to report. The potential paperwork nightmare is such that it becomes an incentive for small firms to stay small since any company with fewer than 50 employees would be exempt from the new proposed regulations.

- In another startling use of executive power, the U.S. signed a United Nations agreement in Paris in 2015 to reduce climate change and intends to implement its responsibilities by executive order. The 2015 agreement with Iran on limiting its nuclear capabilities was treated in the same way — executive implementation with no need for Congressional participation.

This change in the way the federal government operates, happening before our eyes, is exacerbated by Congressional behavior. It has declined, for example, to take action to limit Presidential power to wage war unilaterally in the Middle East. One former Assistant Attorney General for National Security put it this way: "Congress has abdicated its role, deferring to the executive branch rather than take on a potentially controversial issue."

THE STATES

Part of the checks and balances has to do with how states implement laws that involve their jurisdictions. A state refusing to accept a federal program effectively stymies the program in that state. For the most part, the feds have used monetary incentives to secure the compliance to national programs. For example, President Eisenhower famously wanted a national highway system to match the German autobahns. So his administration told the states that if they agreed to build highways in their jurisdictions according to a set of federal standards — and to link those highways seamlessly to similar highways being built by neighboring states — the feds would pay 90 percent of the cost. No state could ignore that kind of incentive. Deal done.

Many federal laws, of course, are strongly resisted by the states. The issue of nullification, in fact, was one of the transfiguring issues leading to the Civil War. Because of the Constitution's 10th Amendment —

> . . . *powers not delegated to the United States . . . are reserved to the States . . . or to the people* —

the tradition of resistance to federal intrusion into the business of the states continues into the 21st century.

One recent example involved illegal immigrants. They are specifically *ineligible* for the benefits of the Affordable Care Act. Nevertheless, 20 of the 25 largest counties in the U.S. provide illegal immigrants with medical services as if they were eligible for Obamacare. These jurisdictions point out that it is far cheaper for them to give *preventive* medical services to people rather than treat them after they become ill. It should be noted that as this book went to press, none of the counties defying the law in this way has suffered any negative consequences. It is unlikely they will during the Obama administration. But respect for the law in a country that proclaims itself a country of laws suffers when lobbycratic governance decides which laws to obey and which ones to ignore.

THE U.S. GOVERNMENT IN REALITY

All this illustrates that the whole U.S. federal

government no longer works as it was originally conceived. Rather than a government of, by and for the people — as Lincoln so eloquently described it at the end of the Gettysburg Address — we now have a national government in which the people are essentially superfluous to its decision-making.

- Its parts are managed by legislative and administrative technocrats working in conjunction with lobbyists representing special interest groups. These groups provide the financing that keeps elected officials largely compliant with the groups' goals.

- The need to compromise in order to govern the country shattered around the turn of the 21st century. Democrats insist that government serve as a compassionate provider of last resort to those unable to provide for themselves; Republicans see government involvement in the lives of citizens as part of the problem rather than the solution. As the more liberal and conservative fringes of both parties move into positions of greater influence within the House and Senate, the chasm that separates the parties has become even more pronounced. The stronger the left and right wings of each party becomes in each successive election cycle, the chances for meaningful compromise on key societal issues lessens.

The disagreement over filling the vacancy created by the death of Associate Supreme Court Justice Antonin Scalia provides a dramatic example of the split between left and right philosopsies in the United States. As noted above, Democrats have called for prompt Senate hearings on selecting a successor. But knowing that any Obama nominee is likely to give the four sitting liberal justices a fifth ally on key social and economic issues, the Republican leadership has insisted that the post be left vacant so a new President can select a successor in 2017.

The truth is that if the American government ever came close to functioning in a way that could be described as of, by and for the people, it is far from that ideal now. In fact the notion that the Federal government operates for the benefit of ordinary citizens has come under an enormous cloud in the 2016 presidential election. That said, Americans are still hard pressed to give up on the Lincolnian ideal. While a government of, by and for the people may be scoffed at by some, it also means that a large group of citizens hope that Lincoln's dream may yet come true.

As a result, many Americans chose to believe in an elaborate fairy tale about how their government works. The fairy tale may also be preventing a lot of people from getting involved in trying to repair what others see as broken. Moreover, how can ordinary people hope to fix something that they believe was put together by divinely inspired geniuses? So nothing necessary to fix the government tends to happen from year to year. No proposals are discussed to offset the increasing power of lobbyists to affect the way technocrats massage the rules and interpret the regulations — all for the benefit of a small number of big organizations, corporations and institutions.

Most Americans really *want* to believe in the fairy tale because it seems so logical, so neat and ultimately so fair — much like the America of Norman Rockwell's illustrations, of the outcome of the film *Mr. Smith Goes to Washington*, and of the mood of the TV series *Father Knows Best*.

But something vital has always been missing from their tidy description of how America operates. For one thing, there is a bedrock belief in the separation of church and state. To most, the words "In God we trust" on coinage or "under God" added to the Pledge of Allegiance don't violate the division. From their point of view, no harm is done since all major religions accept a Supreme Being. But to atheists the opening prayer before each session of the House and Senate violates the separation between church and state.

Rather than resolve the issue in open debate, the tendency is to ridicule those who object and to accept the view of the vast majority in favor. But it is these unresolved issues that lead to deep societal divisions. By the same token, high school teachers and immigration instructors spend most of their time with students on the *mechanics* of American government — when elections are conducted, how the veto power works, the number of justices on the Supreme Court. It is as if the answers to these questions describe the reality of American government.

As a consequence, almost no time is devoted to the *fuel* that keeps the American government running.

Missing are the two topics that actually determine how any governmental function will be carried out from start to finish:

MONEY AND POLITICS.

There is generally only sporadic mention of these two aspects of governance. There is little consideration of how they interact in the simplistic descriptions of how the U.S. government works.

The oft given reason for the absence of these two topics in basic discussions of American government is that politics and its relationship to money are not mentioned in the Constitution. Fair enough, but that doesn't mean they aren't vital elements of the fabric of American governmental life. The symbiotic connection of politics and money in the United States is at the heart of what needs to be done to change American governance in the future.

Every two years America's citizens face the same two questions in every election:

1. What do we want our government to do for us and others — the things we can't do for ourselves or as efficiently; and

2. How are these activities to be paid for and in what amounts?

THE DO'S AND THE DON'T'S
There is no agreement on the answers to these two fundamental questions even though answers are sought every two years. The reason may well be the gulf that has formed between what one group calls the "doers" of society and the rest of the population. The difference may not be entirely accurate,

but it gains credence as it circulates on the Internet. One such piece declares that there are actually *two* Americas:

- The America that works, and the America that doesn't.

- The America that contributes, and the America that doesn't.

- It's not the have's and the have not's any more, but the do's and the don'ts. Some people *do* their duty as American citizens, obey the laws, support themselves and contribute to society; others *don't*.

The doers, for the most part, are conservatives; the don'ts cluster on the progressive side. The differences between the two can be seen in these perceived policy absurdities:

- Plastic water *bottles* are okay in every jurisdiction in the country, but plastic *bags* are now banned in many.

- You can get arrested for hunting or fishing without a license, but not for entering the country illegally.

- You must show identification to board an airplane, cash a check, buy liquor, register at a hotel, but not to vote for those who collect and spend our tax money.

- Hard work and success are met with higher taxes and more government regulation, while *not* working is rewarded with SNAP (Supplemental Nutrition Assistance Program

— the old food stamps — delivered now on electronic debit cards), WIC (Women, Infants and Children) checks, Medicaid benefits, subsidized housing, and free cell phones.

The gulf between the two groups has led to a decision by the self-proclaimed doers of society to look out more aggressively for their own interests. Government can no longer be trusted to be fair and equitable to all. The upshot is that many of the "doers" have sought "outsider" candidates to change the direction of government; others have begun engaging well-paid lobbyists to work with senior technocrats and elected politicians to find solutions to problems that serve *their* needs. They are no longer concerned with everyone else.

THE BIGS

As a result, the United States government has now become an arena where the BIGS clash — not the very large athletes at the center and forward positions of National Basketball Association and national Olympic teams, but the economic, social and cultural BIGS of such entities as:

- Big industrial corporations
- Big retailers
- Big Internet players
- Big Wall Street brokerage houses
- Big hedge funds
- Big banks
- Big financial bundlers

- Big labor unions
- Big universities
- Big think tanks
- Big media
- Big political action committees
- Big charities
- Big law firms
- Big accounting firms
- Big pharmaceutical houses
- Big insurance providers
- Big entertainment personalities
- Big celebrity names
- Big philanthropists
- And big in every other category.

If you aren't part of something BIG, you aren't effectively participating in the *politics* of today.

The difference between the BIGS and the rest of us was well illustrated in a political cartoon dealing with California's multi-year drought. The artist portrays Governor Jerry Brown talking out of two sides of his mouth. To bleak looking average citizens he is saying "Kill your lawn . . . cap your hose . . . cut your water use by 25%." On the other side of the frame is a well-dressed, cigar smoking figure in the form of a pig with a sign that reads "80% of the water, 2% of the economy." Brown is saying to this character labeled BIG Agriculture: "I am not going to be Big Brother and tell you what to do."

If you can't comfortably attach yourself politically to some aspect of the BIG culture, you won't be wealthy enough to succeed — individually or collectively. If you aren't rich enough, you can't contribute meaningfully to political campaigns, to do the research to support your point of view, to conduct public opinion polls and focus groups to justify your position for any kind of government project or undertaking. That means that changing America becomes a much more difficult and challenging proposition.

- The BIGS have enormous influence over the selection of candidates for election at all levels of government by virtue of the amount of money they can commit to election campaigns. Without funding for name recognition, for publication of campaign material, for full-time staff support, for paid advertising, for extensive travel and for personal expenses, most candidacies flounder.

- The BIGS are the only ones that can afford to engage particular law firms who have hired former senior government officials who know how to push the right buttons or pull the right strings within the executive branch, on legislative committees or in regulatory agencies to get matters stopped, delayed or moving.

  The principals of these law firms are now charging in excess of $1,000 per hour(!) for their time — and most of the hours prove to be shy of a full 60 minutes in terms of productive output. There are interruptions for the questions of colleagues, for phone calls from family, tweets on topics of interest, for bathroom breaks, coffee breaks, snack breaks, and for all the other diversions that occur without the clock ever really stopping. Those kinds of fees make the law firms BIG and their very bigness allows them to increase their influence as they hire senior technocrats and retiring lawmakers from all points along the political continuum at generous salaries with attractive perks.

- The BIGS provide contracts to the think tanks, grants to university professors, and tasks to polling firms to produce the facts, research and analysis that greatly influence the laws shepherded by elected officials and the rules adopted by the technocrats. Since the BIGS hire other BIGS to further justify their expense reports, there is a tendency for all of them to see the world through similar lenses.

- The BIGS provide the jobs in the private sector that technocrats and former politicians covet as their kids enter university and they see the disparity between what government offers in pay and benefits and what some elements of the private sector can deliver.

- On many issues, the BIGS get the benefit of the doubt from the technocrats for no other reason than their very BIGNESS suggests the ability to develop, persist and sustain a viable point of view. The tendency to respect the BIGS for their BIGNESS provides a subtle tilt when not all the facts mesh, when not all the justifications are solid, and when support seems mushy. That keeps the BIGS in business, ensures their continuing prosperity, and generates the belief in their future potential as a source for a technocrat's employment in the private sector.

REAL MONEY

Given the fact that lobbyists for the BIGS and technocrats in Congress and the executive branch are so tightly lashed together, exactly what are elected officials doing for their salaries? They sure aren't doing much *legislating*.

Instead they are making sure that those problems their *constituents* may encounter with government are resolved. Look at some Congressional offices and you see large staffs of case workers. They are also acting as major facilitators to make sure that issues important to one or more of the BIGS in their home districts are drafted into legislation and eventually supported by favorable implementing rules.

- How else did the Affordable Care Act get approved? After all, it was a 2,700-page bill, designed and lobbied by the big insurance companies and supported by big pharma. It mandated health benefits for those who had been denied them or who couldn't afford them. The bill was so big in its scope, so dense in its references, and so complex in its caveats that the Speaker of the House of Representatives famously said that it had to be passed in order to find out what was in it. What Nancy Pelosi meant, of course, is that the words in the law don't count as much as the wording of the rules that implement the law — and only when both law and regulations have operated over time can it be determined if everything is working as all the BIGS intended.

- How else does a 1,530-page, $3.6 trillion, 2014 federal budget come to the floor of the House for a final vote just two days after it was *printed* as a whole and then moved through the Senate one day later? Who actually wrote the provisions of that bill that become law and binding on all Americans? Who read it critically enough to understand exactly what was being enacted? Since no one could have read, absorbed and commented on that mass of data in such a short period of time, it is reasonable to assume that only technocrats and their lobbyist colleagues knew what was actually in parts of the bill as it was being assembled, provision by provision. Yet some very real money — like $3.6 trillion worth of real money[†] — was committed for a lot of questionable activities.

[†]Pause a moment. How much real money is involved in $3,600,000,000,000? When reduced to the convenience of writing or saying three point six trillion, maybe it doesn't seem so much, particularly compared to the Fiscal Year 2016 budget of $4.1 tril-

Wouldn't you think that spending that kind of money might require a little more thought than a couple of days? Well, it does, of course, but little of the thought is expended by elected officials with responsibility for doing so. It is applied by lobbyists working with government technocrats. They are deciding how income from tax dollars and the enormous sums borrowed by the Treasury Department are being spent on roads and medicine and weapons and schools and a lot more for the ensuing year.

LOBBYCRATIC GOVERNANCE ELSEWHERE

At the state level, the system works even more in favor of the lobbyists and the technocrats in the absence of aggressive news media reporting. There, too, politicians have to contend with the possibility that unlimited contributions will be made to their next election opponent as well as face the conse-

---

lion. The numbers roll off the tongue easily — listen to any anchor read their teleprompters. But when people actually realize the enormity of a trillion dollars they pause. One trillion is a *million* million or a *thousand* billion. For comparison, the largest university endowment in the world is "only" $36 billion. Look at it another way: Banks receive new $100 bills from the Federal Reserve in packets that consist of 100 stacks. These packets amount to $10,000 and are about one-half inch thick each. It takes 100 of these packets to make $1 million — that stack measures about four feet high. A *thousand* of those stacks equals $1 billion. But 1,000 stacks require 10 pallets to move around. A trillion dollars would takes *1,000* pallets — enough to cover a warehouse floor. And the U.S. goes through the equivalent of nearly *4,000* of these pallets each year!

quences of term limits. Term limits were passed in many states because government in the state capitals seemed controlled by an old-boy network. By limiting the number of years a person could serve in a single office, proponents thought fresh faces would bring fresh ideas to their legislatures. It didn't.

The law of unintended consequences set in. Term limits created a class of politicians with little grasp of the intricacies of legislative rules and governmental procedures. The technocrats and lobbyists moved into this void. They provided guidance for elected officials on the technicalities of the process. Soon most of these newly minted office holders thought why master that stuff if someone else knows it and if I am only going to have a few years to use the learning before moving on?

This of course made those politicians even more dependent on the permanent class of government specialists in the capitals of each state — the lobbyists and the technocrats working in the halls and offices of state capitols. The lobbyist has become the institutional memory for legislators new to the task, guiding the politicians as to how things have always been done and of course funding the compliant politician's next campaign as he is pushed by term limits up the political ladder toward higher office.

Because of the way government operates today, most elected officials have one of two new roles.

- The politicians with an interest in doing something to change societal directions or a penchant for public policy become *enablers* for the lobbyists and technocrats in their states. Once a general consensus on a new policy direction has been developed with the elder statesmen of various economic and social sectors and endorsed by the media and the university thinkers in the jurisdiction, the lobbyists and technocrats go to work to write the actual legislation to implement the policy.

- The politicians who worry primarily about constituent problems with government agencies — lost welfare benefits, missing car titles, traffic bottlenecks, and the like — become *concierges*. They make sure they have good relations with the governor's staff and with the departmental executives in the governor's administration. Their contacts provide the names within the bureaucracies and the introductions for constituents to solve whatever problem has been presented to them.

SUMMARY

Lobbyists, technocrats and politicians constitute the new *troika* controlling American governance at the national, state and big city levels. As a tight group with a lot of personal prestige, power and money at stake, they tend to circle the wagons at every sign of public disaffection — or when books like this threaten to cause dissatisfaction with their stewardship of government.

They then spend a lot of the public's money to deny an accusation, challenge an assumption, defend a colleague or change the subject. This leaves the people to pick up the pieces for the mistakes the troika makes. These pieces are manifested in the higher licensing fees that cause prices to rise, the lawsuit settlements that blame an institutional malfunction rather than the malfeasance of an administrator, the deficits left by purposefully underfunded programs, the search for non-existent weapons of mass destruction, the rising costs of Obamacare insurance premiums in the face of reduced competition, and much more.

But every time you are inclined to leave solutions to these types of problems to others, remember this story of governmental excess reported in the *Los Angeles Times* in March 2016. The sheriff of Santa Clara County in California asked her Board of Supervisors to authorize the installation of surveillance cameras in the main jail. The Supervisors agreed and gave the task to their technocrats who, in turn, asked lobbyists for contractors likely to engineer the system, buy the equipment and install the cameras and computers, to plan the system.

The estimate came back that it would take two years to design and install the camera system and would cost $20 million. The sheriff was appalled. The next day she went to Costco, the giant big box discounter, discussed her need with a floor salesman, bought 12 cameras and a digital video recorder, and put the $741 cost on her credit card. A jail maintenance crew got the equipment up and running in one of the wings of the jail as a demonstration in a day or two.

Lucky thing. The next day, a riot broke out in

module and it was all caught on the new cameras and recorder — brought in 719 days ahead of schedule and at a savings to taxpayers of $19,999,259. Not bad when someone is willing to take responsibility away from the lobbyists, technocrats and politicians to get things done.

3.
ROAD MAP

As you clearly realize at this point, the thesis of this book is that the United States government now operates differently from ways that the couyntry was controlled through most of the 20th century. Between the founding of the nation and the Eisenhower administration, most Americans believed in an American creed of individualism, equality and opportunity; then three events in a 10-year period fundamentally changed the attitude of most Americans toward their government:

1. President John F. Kennedy was assassinated in Dallas in November 1963 at the outset of

his campaign for election to a second term to complete the program of the New Frontier.

2. The Vietnam War, a conflict in a country few Americans had heard of and even fewer cared about, suddenly went from the fringes of America's conscience to the center of public concern. Why? America's leaders argued that unless the Communist tide spilling across Southeast Asia was halted, it could topple governments one after another like falling dominoes — in Indochina, Indonesia, the Philippines and perhaps Australia. This-would endanger the United States. Because the military draft touched every male over the age of 18 at the time, the war became very real as more and more men were conscripted, others sought deferments, and ever greater amounts of borrowed money was consumed.

   And to what end? To fight battles in a jungle environment against what many at home perceived as a ragtag enemy? Why hadn't the U.S. dispatched such an enemy as it had much more imposing forces in World War II? The disconnect between the country's leadership and its people grew ever more pronounced. Most Americans didn't understand the purpose of the war and most soon came to doubt its necessity to *their* country's well-being.

3. After the shock of Kennedy's death and the venomous attitude toward Lyndon Johnson and the escalating Vietnam War, Richard Nixon came to the presidency. But after the opening to China, he got caught up in some

seriously illegal activities linked to his 1972 reelection campaign. It eventually forced him to become the first U.S. president to resign from office.

The American body politic changed dramatically after three cataclysmic political events occurred in the space of a decade — the sudden end of a popular and promising young President's life; a widely hated, ever-enlarging war that sucked up so many lives; and the resignation of a complicated, venal President.

These three events were the political equivalent of a shift of tectonic plates — significant enough to destroy the basically positive attitude most Americans had toward their government. But there was more. The economy suffered from Johnson's insistence that the country could pay for the war *and* the enormous number of Great Society programs without any increase in taxes.

This dogged approach created inflationary forces that pushed a lot of women back into the work force and fostered a feminist revolution that decreed they would have equality with men in every area of human endeavor. They set out to do for themselves what a male-dominated government and a male-dominated society had failed to do. Seeing their success, the gay community soon began its own push for equality in all aspects of life.

Lobbycratic governance grew out of these enormous changes and has gained strength over the ensuing 40 years. It wasn't planned and it hadn't been authorized; but its evolution and the acceptance of its consequences have altered the way society now deals with its problems and challenges. When most people realize the state of play in government today and how little real influence they have in how government actually affects their lives, many are concerned, some become agitated, and a few want to do something about it.

Putting a precise date on when the lobbycratic state became strong enough to be recognized as the dominant mechanism governing America is probably impossible from our current vantage point. It is clear, however, that one event gave significant impetus to creating the current way in which our government actually operates. It was the 2010 Supeme Court decision in the case of:

Citizens United v. Federal Election Commission.

The case arose because a conservative lobbying group called Citizens United wanted to advertise and show a derogatory film called *Hillary: The Movie* before a 2008 primary election. The group had formed as a tax deductible nonprofit organization under Section 501(c)(4) of the Internal Revenue Code. That section allows "social welfare groups" to engage in civic activities, but unlike a 501(c)(3) group, contributions are *not* tax deductible. Significantly, though, the identify of contributors to 501(c)(4) organizations can be kept hidden from public view.

Under the McCain-Feingold campaign finance law, the Federal Election Commission held that such a film was prohibited as an "electioneering communication" when shown within 60 days of a general election or 30 days of a primary election. The Commission also found that advertising and showing the film involved prohibited expenditures by corporations and unions.

The Citizens United organization challenged the ruling in court, arguing that prohibiting corporations or unions from involvement in a political campaign was a denial of *their* freedom of speech rights. In a 5 to 4 decision, the Supreme Court held that provisions of McCain-Feingold prohibiting corporations and unions from making independent expenditures and engaging in "electioneering communications" was unconstitutional. One of the key findings in the Court's ruling was that the "electioneering communications" of corporations and unions had to be completely independent of the activities of the candidates and their official campaigns. The Court left standing the prohibition on direct corporate and union contributions to a *candidate*.

That opinion was a bombshell. It galvanized large organizations and rich individuals into using their enormous resources to influence government policy through the ballot box. As a result, some members of Congress effectively gave up on their historic *policy making* role to the point that Senator Mike Lee, a Republican of Utah, noted:

> *Congress has recast itself as a back-seat driver in American politics.*

To counter this trend, a group associated with Senator Lee created the "Article 1 Project." This activity has set about to try to reverse *Citizens United* and recover some of the authority that Congress has ceded to the executive branch and the independent regulatory agencies. In a policy paper, the Article 1 Project has declared that:

> *Congress willfully shirks [its] responsibility and ... often encourages the executive branch to do work the Constitution assigns to the legislature. Congress's refusal to use its powers — to do its duty — is the root cause of Washington's dysfunction and of the public scorn it invites.*

As an example of why Congress no longer exercises its Article 1 powers as forcefully as before, two senators point to the unwillingness of the leadership to set a vote on authorizing a declaration of war on the Islamic State.

If there is no vote, no member of Congress can be held accountable for an activity that turns out badly. When Congress refuses to act, the administration is on its own.

Of course, once power is relinquished from one branch of government to another, it is difficult to get it back. Do they even want it back? Senator Lee asserts that Congress has forsaken its authority partly to dodge tough decisions and make it easier for lawmakers to be re-elected with unblemished records.[†]

By not exerting itself on difficult issues, Congress

[†]An unblemished record is not always a good thing. Modern military leaders are advanced through the ranks primarily because there are no "blots on their copybooks." But in having spent aa

creates a vacuum that is filled by other powerful groups. Active, wealthy and policy-oriented groups led the rise of the lobbycratic state.

An interesting set of statistics suggests why lobbycratic governance grew so quickly. In the 18 presidencies prior to Obama's, the number of cabinet members thought to have significant business experience averaged about 45 percent.

In the Obama cabinet only 8 percent have had any serious business experience, with the rest coming from positions in government, academia and nonprofit organizations. What is significant is not the raw numbers, but the fact that Mr. Obama's cabinet contains 82 percent fewer business people than the average number in the cabinets of his predecessors. If nothing else, this suggests the dominance that technocrats have achieved at the very highest levels of American government.

This book is about helping those who want to see a change in this trajectory. To do so requires:

- An understanding of recent developments that affect governance;

- How American governance actually works today; and

- How it can be returned to functioning more like a government of, by and for the people.

---

career taking no risks and avoiding being responsible for any mistakes, these officers become the polar opposite of such military leaders as Douglas MacArthur, George Patton or Norman Schwarzkopf. Bland does not win battles or wars; it only prolongs bureaucratic careers.

To accomplish these three tasks, the following chapters provide statistical revelations, relevant examples, anecdotal evidence, case studies and new ideas for possible implementation. These next chapters look at national and local issues and events that are designed to be read or sampled to appreciate the flavor of so many different political currents flowing in the same direction.

In short, we hope that this book from this point forward will stimulate people to:

Get the drift, get agitated, and then get started in having a role in getting things right.

4.
THE ASCENDANCY OF LOBBYING

The influence of lobbying on legislation and regulation did not suddenly arise when *Citizens United* was decided in 2010. Lobbying political bodies to achieve a desired end has existed since the beginning of the republic. It was guaranteed by the right of petition in the First Amendment to the Constitution. But lobbyists have gained more and more influence as voter distrust of government has intensifiedover the years. Even with the Kennedy assassination, the quagmire of the Vietnam War and the Watergate scandal, the United States government did not stop operating and its programs did not stop absorbing mountains of money.

As long as government was in a position to provide help to the private sector — with massive contracts, supportive funds or through restrictive laws and regulations — there were lobbyists eager to direct the money to their clients or the regulations against any business that could be considered a competitor of their clients.

LOBBYISTS

Lobbyists of former days actually loitered around the hallways and lounges outside of the legislative chambers. They were there to make contact with elected members, bringing them fresh information or relevant news of mutual interest — and sometimes special rewards. The hope, of course, was that the contact would be instrumental in influencing the outcome of pending legislation. As the nature of government changed, so did the focus of lobbyists.

When legislators began employing staff to assist them in their work, lobbyists began to befriend, help and try to influence key staff members on behalf of their causes or employers. When executive branch agencies started their ascendancy to power, lobbyists began to cultivate the officials running the agencies. But when dealing with executive branch organizations, the lobbyists focused on the regulations that dictated how any aspect of policy was to be interpreted and implemented.

Soon lobbyists and those who most often dealt with them moved into executive positions in key government agencies:

- Of the 36 individuals that Barack Obama has

appointed to his cabinet over the eight years of his presidency, *all* have been involved with lobbyists and their causes. This includes the 16 who were government technocrats before entering the cabinet, the 15 who are professional politicians, and the three who came from predominantly business backgrounds.

- In California, openings in the five member Fish and Wildlife Commission — the policy-making agency charged with writing the regulations that are enforced by the Department of Fish and Wildlife — have been filled by representatives of animal interventionist groups. This has happened as the number of hunters and anglers has dwindled below 1 percent of the population. As such, the agency has been transformed from one *preserving* wildlife in California to one intent on *conserving* it. As an example of the change, California issued a little more than 600,000 hunting licenses when its population was 22 million in the 1970s. By 2015, it issued only 272,000 licenses to a population of 39 million!

The lobbyists in Washington and in state capitals soon grew to corps-level strength. Here is how the Sunlight Foundation, a nonprofit group dedicated to informing the public on the workings of government, put it in late 2013:

> *The lobbying industry is so big [and shadowy] that Washington's . . . economy seems to have weathered the economic storm of recent years.*[†]

The reason for the lack of transparency is clear: the Lobbying Disclosure Act's definition of "lobbyist" is too narrow. If lobbyists want, they can fully comply with the law and do virtually the same influence-for-pay as strategic policy consultants or historical advisers, and choose not to disclose [themselves or their work.] Even lobbyists . . . seem to find little meaning in the term "lobbyist." The American League of Lobbyists . . . dropped the word "lobbyist" from their name to officially become the Association of Government Relations Professionals.

James Thurber, head of the Center for Presidential and Congressional Studies at American University, believes the real number of those who are engaged in influencing the way the U.S. government operates is closer to 90,000. Equally startling is the number of congressional senior staffers who formerly were registered lobbyists. Their number doubled between the 111th and 112th Congress.

Whatever the actual number, lobbyists spend a ton of money.

If we assume that the cost of reported and stealth lobbying is the same—that every one person accounts for . . . about $270,000 in lobbying [cost] per year — then we estimate that in the calendar year 2012, organized interests spent about $6.7 billion "relating" with the government.

---

†Despite the enormity of the lobbying industry in Washington, no one is quite sure exactly how many lobbyists and other influence peddlers are plying the Washington scene on any given day or on behalf of any number of clients or issues.

The Foundation put that number into perspective by comparing it to the cost of each Congressional office.

> *For every member of Congress, the influence industry [spent] about $12.5 million in lobbying costs. By comparison, the average 2012 budget for a member of the House of Representative's office was only $1.3 million. So, in 2012—a presidential election year, in a down economy, during arguably the least productive Congress ever—"government relaters" consumed more than nine times the typical House member's official operating expenses.*

While this is an interesting comparison, it is important to remember that much more significant lobbying now goes on across executive branch agencies rather than among members of Congress. Here are some numbers along these lines.

> *. . . the one-year $6.7 billion tally [for lobbying] is about $500 million more than all the campaign money spent [during] the record-setting 2012 election cycle. So if we multiply the one-year lobbying industry estimate by two years, then the . . . [opaque] lobbying industry inside the Beltway [spent] about twice [the funds] of the relatively highly regulated campaign finance system that influences politics outside the Beltway.*

Absorbing this one statistic should be enough to demonstrate that America is a lobbycratic nation. Consider another example: Chemical companies alone spent the equivalent of $100,000 per member of the House and Senate in 2015. Their money was aimed at making sure that the government did not put in place any serious oversight of the chemical industry. The result, Nicholas Kristoff wrote in *The New York Times*, is that —

> *. . . almost none of the chemical products we use daily have been tested for safety.*

Some months later, *The Wall Street Journal* reported that organizations representing such chemical industry biggies as Dow and DuPont orchestrated a chemical safety bill that preempted states and even private companies from interfering with federal safety evaluations. The bill passed the House 403 to 12, suggesting that the chemical companies were comfortable with the process they had devised. Had the suggested procedures been too restrictive or burdensome, we likely would have seen the House split along party lines. We will have to wait to see who feels unhappy with the new law when it becomes fully operational.

Each house of Congress has implemented rules for lobbyists and require their registration. But since many in the influence business do their work quietly and far from Capitol Hill, registration may be all show and no substance.

> There are so many lobbyists spilling out across the government that even the lobbyists have sought ways to distinguish their concerns from others. Take the case of Mike Brown, chief Senate lobbyist for the city of Washington. Although he calls himself "Senator" Michael Brown of the District of Columbia,

House side. There, the members have welcomed an official delegate from the District and provided her with all the accoutrements of office including membership on important House committees and the right to engage in floor debate.

Although the District employs Brown, it does so as a *lobbyist* rather than as a member of what used to be called the Most Exclusive Club in the world. Despite the Senatorial title that Brown has adopted, he has no special privileges on Capitol Hill. As a shadow senator (in the same sense that opposition politicians "shadow" the work and policies of government ministers in a parliamentary system), Brown works with the D.C. mayor, its council and the House delegate to advance the interests of local residents on federal issues.

LOBBYING TECHNIQUES

As readers by now know, American government is today about lobbying and technocrats.[†] Having noted the fundamental points about lobbycratic governance, recognize that lobbyists are not all of

---

[†]Money gives lobbyists their enormous clout. Note this April 2016 Email from Senator Elizabeth Warren to masses of Americans who have previously given money to MoveOn.org:

> On Thursday, I met with Chief Judge Merrick Garland, President Obama's Supreme Court nominee. [M]y friends at MoveOn.org [have a] new, bold strategy to break the Republican blockade on his nomination. [T]hey have their eye on one senator who's at the center of the ... fight. And they have a plan that . . . could work to bring that senator around— and start a domino effect that leads to hearings and an up-or-down vote . . .
>
> To make it work, MoveOn is going to launch a powerful campaign targeting that one Senate Republican. But they need to raise $150,000 [in 48

the same stripe. There are lobbyists representing organizations, institutions and corporations on every side of every major issue. Depending on how the winds of change are blowing across American society — impacted by economic factors, demographic shifts and philosophical differences — a large organization can be found at any given time either promoting or opposing adjustments in the system.

Here is a hypothetical example of how this occurs in today's world:

> Imagine that a steady influx of new residents speaking an exotic East Asian dialect have recently moved into the same neighborhood in a large urban area. Their kids are doing poorly in the local schools because they do not understand the instruction being presented in English. One of the established members of the community, having learned how American government works, gets in touch with a civil rights group about the problem. The group in turn gets in

---

hours] to pull it off. Can you help out? The Republicans are turning one of the most solemn and consequential decisions that U.S. senators make into a partisan circus. It's utterly unprecedented. And we simply can't let them get away with it. But we need your help to make it work.

The appeal is geared to support an undefined campaign either aimed at an unidentified candidate or for an undisclosed purpose. The hidden message from one of the Internet's biggest political BIGs is "trust us" to persuade elected officials to do the right thing. It represents a clear, up-to-date example of how lobbycratic governance works in a democratic setting that essentially removes the people from the government that ostensibly works for them.

touch with the local office of a Congressman. The group demands federal funds to support a new translator for the elementary schools. The civil rights group figures its involvement is a win-win situation. They win if the Congressman's office produces the translator and they win in terms of getting fresh donations from their followers to sustain a lawsuit if it doesn't.

In the old days, the congressman might have called his contact in the office of the cabinet secretary to make a pitch for assistance. It would have been handled in a few days — either finding the needed funds in an established program or reserve account or turning down the request pending the next budget cycle.

Today, these kinds of matters are handled by technocrats. That means that someone in the Washington office of the congressman meets with a functionary in the Department of Education. Together they discuss what federal programs might already apply to satisfy the request. Once they have settled on a path forward, lobbyists for teachers, administrators and language specialists are alerted by both the Congressman's office and the executive agency to how the changes being discussed might impact programs their members favor.

The last thing a congressman wants to do is annoy these groups, They represent large campaign donations and an important bloc of votes. To embarrass them or hide something from them would have negative consequences.

Soon emails are exchanged, position papers are drafted, multiple meetings are arranged, a decision memo is prepared, a speech announcing the decision is drafted, and a suitable venue and date are selected for the big reveal. While delay is possible for budgetary reasons, outright denial is not likely when so many voices are invited to be in the discussion. The usual item left out of these discussions is how the cost of the program should be funded.

Just as soon as the technocrats and lobbyists have finished their work, the member of Congress is briefed on what has been agreed and how he needs to inform his colleagues of the arrangement. Meanwhile, the high level agency technocrats are doing the same thing — briefing their political leadership on what is coming.

When a critical mass of voices, representing influential individuals, big money interests and a substantial number of votes are on the same side, the issue is either approved for implementation or postponed to a point in the future.[†]

This hypothetical example shows how an issue becomes a task for the technocrats and lobbyists to deal with. This scenario plays out in countless real life dramas every day in Washington, Albany, Austin, Annapolis, Atlanta and many other state

---

[†]Nothing in Washington is ever killed or dies; it is just rendered dormant while the forces opposed or in favor assess their next move or study the terrain for another try at some point in the future when circumstances are likely to have changed.

capitals. In fact, there is usually so much of consequence going on involving lobbyists and the special interest groups they work for that these two *real life* examples of lobbycratic governance was reported on the same day in 2016 in the *Los Angeles Times*:

> **Obamacare**. Doctors, clinics and pharmacies buy the medicine that patients need and then get reimbursed by Medicare. Medicare pays the provider at its cost plus 6 percent profit. Long before Medicare Part B was created, the cost-plus contract was a favorite device in defense work. While inserted innocently enough in contracts to cover uncharted territory and unforeseen problems that weaponry development often entailed, it soon became an easy way to raise employee wages, pay whatever price a seller demanded, and result in making a bigger profit for the company in the process.
>
> Adopting the payment technique to pharmaceuticals may have had the same rationale, but it also provided the same manipulative opportunities. It didn't take long for some to figure out that the higher the cost of a medicine from a pharmaceutical firm or provider, the more real dollars the 6 percent fee could yield to the pharmacies and the prescribing physicians.
>
> As a result, when the Obama administration proposed a change in this payment formula, big pharma had a fit. The administration said it wanted to provide more incentives

to choose the most *effective* medicine for the patient, not necessarily the one *costing* the most. That suggestion was greeted with the usual strongly worded, self-righteous objection that defend an accepted economic principle rather than the details of a specific drug program. Here is what Big Pharma told the world about the Obama Administration's proposed change:

> *[The current Part B system is] an effective, market-based pricing mechanism that works to control costs.*

Except when it doesn't. Chemotherapy treatments, for example, more than doubled in cost between 2005 and 2012 due mostly to price increases rather than any changes in formulations or ingredients. So far, cost-plus contracts still prevail in Washington.

Smoking. In a second *Los Angeles Times* piece on the same day, lobbyists representing the tobacco industry let fly with a volley of threats related to a California bill that would raise the state's smoking age from 18 to 21 no matter whether the tobacco was inhaled by burning or electronic delivery.

If this bill were to pass and be signed by the governor, the industry said it would immediately place a referendum on the ballot to overturn the measure — pledging to pay signature gathers $10 for each valid name (versus the normal $3 to $5 rate). In the process of throwing its considerable financial weight behind the task of getting a referendum on the ballot, a tobacco industry lobbyist said that another measure heading for the November 2016 ballot — one to do with maintaining a previously approved increase in income taxes along with an increase in the cigarette tax to $2 a pack — would die for lack of professional signature gatherers to get the measure on the ballot.

The threat was issued on behalf of tobacco giant Altria in an email to a legislative staffer. The staffer in turn shared the news with an array of organizations supporting the bill, including the American Lung Association, the California Medical Association, the American Heart Association and the American Cancer Society. They took their frustrations out in a press release:

> *It should come as no surprise that an industry that targets kids for deadly, lifelong addiction would threaten to undermine their education [the beneficiary of the tax measure] and healthcare too. This . . . is a clear indication that the tobacco industry will go to any length to protect a business model that relies on getting kids hoooked on nicotine at an early age.*

This is as good an example as exists of how hardball politics are played in the formation of government policy today. No politicians were in sight or were heard from; no members of the public need comment — the professionals had the matter covered.

Special interest groups, in an era of lobbycratic governance, know that they can get help from government as well as get hurt by it. Here are some examples of lobbying groups that have sought help from government to further their interests.

THE UNIVERSITY OF PHOENIX

There is no better example of the role of lobbyists in a government purportedly of, by and for the people than the case of the University of Phoenix, one of America's principal *for profit* centers of higher learning.

For seven years(!), the Obama administration has tried to curtail these businesses in favor of non-profit universities. The Department of Education has slowly been cutting the federal funding sources of the University of Phoenix. Shares of its parent company have reflected this pressure, pushing its earnings-based price down from a high of $78 to single digits in 2016.

But in politics similar to physics, there is usually a reaction for every action. A Chicago-based private equity firm, seeing the low stock price, began buying shares until it had captured enough to control the University of Phoenix. With the company in hand, the equity firm hired Tony Miller to be its chairman. Although Mr. Miller may not be a household name among even America's political elite, he is well known in educational circles.

He is also an example of why lobbying plays such a major role in how the government *now* works. Mr. Miller had served as the number two official in the Department of Education during President

Obama's first term — and was one of the major architects of the war waged on the for-profit higher education companies.† Here is a portion of what the announcement of Miller's new position said:

> *For too long and too often, the private education industry has been characterized by inadequate student outcomes, overly aggressive marketing practices and poor compliance. This doesn't have to be the case. The University of Phoenix [is committed] to . . . quality higher education for working adults and . . . to operating in a manner consistent with the highest ethical standards.*

Is that right? Why, then, did the Department of Justice and the Department of Education begin investigations of the University of Phoenix in 2015 just after the Department of Defense barred it from "recruiting on military bases." When, asked the *Wall Street Journal,* did "this alleged corporate villain suddenly become dedicated to the welfare of its customers?"

It is not hard to imagine that the transformation started about the time Mr. Miller assumed his new duties. It turns out that the equity fund takeover of the company has to be approved by the Education Department. As is common now in Washington, senior technocrats bounce from government to

---

†Lest readers think that Mr. Miller is alone in lobbying his former agency, note that Marilyn Tavenner is now president and chief executive officer of America's Health Insurance Plans, the trade association for the health insurance industry. Ms. Tavenner is the former administrator of the federal Centers for Medicare and Medicaid Services.

the private sector and back again always ready to work with old friends and perhaps suggest a job or offer a contract whenever a government employee is looking for "a change."

Mr. Miller seems to have fit this mold. A *Journal* editorial summed up this case study in how lobbying really works in Washington today with these words:

> *To summarize, an Obama pal is the day-to-day boss of a department that succeeds in destroying 90% of the value of a politically targeted company. Then he leaves government, buys the company at a fire-sale price and announces that the problems that attracted so much negative government attention are ending — just in time for a new Administration that might not hate for-profit education as much as this one. Government . . . [interference] sure can be a lucrative business model.*

The most distressing aspect of this example of blatant lobbycratic activity is that topics of intense public scrutiny all seem to fade from the public spotlight. In a 24/7 media world that demands a constant supply of fresh information to satisfy myriad special constituencies, topics come as fast as they go. It used to be that weathering a scandal took time; now they are mere squalls that pass through the public conscience rather quickly and seem to do little permanent damage in the process. In short, watch the share price of Apollo Education to see how this story of the University of Phoenix ends.

As stated before, there is little doubt that a sea change in the distribution of power in Washington occurred with the *Citizens United* decision. Recall that this allows corporations and other organizations a Constitutional first amendment right to spend unlimited amounts of money on election-related activities that are independent of any particular candidate or issue campaign.

Former President Jimmy Carter perhaps best explained the impact of *Citizens United* in an interview with the *Guardian* after the Iowa caucuses in 2016. For starters, he said it permitted legalized "bribery."[†] During the Iowa caucuses, Carter said that Republican candidates spent $43 million on TV advertising alone while Democratic candidates spent $16.8 million. Carter said that the domination of money represented the biggest change in American politics since he was elected president in 1976.

I didn't have any money. When I ran against Gerald Ford, or later Ronald Reagan, we didn't raise a single penny to finance our campaigns . . . Now there is a massive infusion of hundreds

---

[†]Well it might. The former governor of Virginia appealed his bribery conviction for accepting cash, vacations and other favors from a Virginia businessman seeking government help for his diet supplement. Governor Bob McDonnell's lawyers based their Supreme Court appeal on a part of the *Citizens United* decision that says "ingratiation and access . . . are not corruption." They argued further that doing small favors for big donors is protected free speech under the first amendment. It turned out that the justices agreed —unanimously. Now a spate of fresh appeals are likely from other politicians convicted of bribery.

of millions of dollars into campaigns for all the candidates. Some candidates . . . have to be able to raise $100 million to $200 million just to get the Republican or Democratic nomination.

He said that *Citizens United* paved the way for superPAC funding vehicles that are being used by big business to buy political influence.

When candidates get in office they do what the rich people want. And that's to let the rich people get richer and richer and the middle class get left out. All the statistics show that the middle class are stagnant or going down in their income for the work that they do.

FANTASY FOOTBALL

Fantasy football has been around for a while, but of late an online competitive version involving substantial amounts of money has grown very large, very quickly. Quite naturally, drawing attention and interest away from other wagering interests raises questions about whether Fantasy Football is a game of skill or chance. The industry argues that it is a game of skill, not chance, and therefore not subject to existing anti-gambling statutes.

But just to be sure its view prevails, the Fantasy Sports Trade Association is coordinating a campaign to protect these games from any new restrictions. So far, the FSTA and its two most prominent members — FanDuel Inc. and DraftKings Inc.— have launched efforts in 34 states involving 78 separate lobbying firms.

The *Wall Street Journal* estimates that the companies

and their trade association will spend between $5 million and $10 million on their effort to specifically exempt fantasy sports from state gambling laws. One analyst noted that if the many bills now pending in the various legislatures become law, the states will have legalized a ton of unregulated and untaxed sports betting. As one analyst noted drily: "I don't think lawmakers get the ramifications of what they are doing."

Not surprising. The same could be said of lawmakers everywhere who become beholden to aggressive lobbyists dedicated to winning for well-funded organizations and corporations. If that means financially supporting a sitting incumbent in his or her next political campaign, fine; if that means finding and funding an opposition candidate in the next election interested in siding with the lobbyist's cause, just as good.

LOBBYING GROUPS AND ELECTIONS
Lobbyists representing deep-pocket organizations also play crucial roles in electoral politics. Getting the right person elected makes influencing how they vote on issues so much easier. In another California example illustrative of this point, millions have been spent on a single seat in the California Assembly. Chevron Corporation, the California Apartment Association and the California Dental Association have backed the incumbent while the Sierra Club and the United Food and Commercial Workers union have funded the challenger. Both candidates are Democrats in a district where no Republican has a prayer of prevailing.

The incumbent in this district, worried about her poor and in many cases unemployed constituents, defied the Democratic establishment by voting against a global warming bill that included phasing out fossil fuels in the state by 2030. That vote enraged the environmentalists who decided to support a workmen's compensation attorney to run against her. The battle between the BIGS is on; each is marshalling an army of people and a ton of printed material to urge a vote for one or the other. of these candidates

The irony in California is that under a recent change in electoral law and because of the current heavy dominance of the Democratic party, the top two finishers in a primary election — regardless of party affiliation — become the run-off candidates in the general election if no one receives 50 percent of the vote.

If politicians have become concierges to facilitate the work of lobbyists and technocrats, then voters often feel like kids in a bounce house — pushed this way and that, day after day, by telephone calls, mailers, pollsters, television commercials, radio spots, and newspaper ads as an election approaches. The interesting result of these kinds of expensive, closely contested election campaigns is that no matter who wins, they know they may have to do it all over again in 24 months.

Just as the military teaches it recruits to reduce their profile in open terrain to present as small a target as possible, so incumbents learn to stick close to their supporters and be immediately responsive to their opponents to reduce the target they offer in subsequent elections. In short, big organizations know that whatever they spend in one election, win or lose, will do them good in a subsequent contest.

EMINENT DOMAIN

Eminent domain is a good example of how the lobbycrats, legislators and lawyers — an alliterative triumvirate — are now working the system for their own benefit. Eminent domain is a long standing legal principal that holds that the state may take private property for a public good. Most people have no problem with the concept when land is required for a major highway, a school expansion or to protect a view. The expectation is that compensation for a "taking" under the 5th and 14th Amendments to the U.S. Constitution is fair and just.

The issue famously became part of the national discussion in 2005 in th famous *Kelso v. City of New London*. This small Connecticut town condemned a man's private waterfront property to allow a developer to build a shopping center on the land. At issue was the question of whether it was permissible for the *government to* take privately owned land from one individual to give to another on the grounds that the new owner will make a greater economic contribution to the community as a result.

The U.S. Supreme Court held in another 5 to 4 decision that furthering economic development by creating jobs qualified private redevelopment plans as a permissible "public use" even if the developer stood to make a lot of money in the process. The tragic irony of the Kelso case is that once the condemnation issue had been resolved by the Supreme Court, the private developer was unable to obtain the financing needed for his project. No shopping center was built; no jobs created for the community. The land was left as an empty lot, a reminder of the greed, insensitivity and uncaring attitudes of technocrats, lobbyists and politicians, aided by the legal profession, exercising governmental power to enhance their careers, their earning potential and their retirement funds. The public was again out of frame on this question.

THE REVOLVING DOOR

As noted above in the case of Phoenix University's Tony Miller, one of the great challenges in conquering the grip that lobbycrats have on the operation of American government involves the relationship between lobbying groups and the major bureaucracies. It is often described as a revolving door between the private and public sectors in which people pass from a job in one to a job in another.

It works this way. An individual starts in the bureaucracy at an entry level position but soon exits to take a private sector job doing lobbying duty with his or her old government agency. Eventually the individual re-enters the same bureaucracy at a much high level than would have been the case if the individual had stayed put and been promoted in the normal course of events.

In and out, back and forth, gaining ever more power to the point that these individuals are rightfully called lobbycrats. Along the way, the individual learns the culture of both groups, how power is apportioned, and what interests each group zealously protects. Equally important, the individual ends up climbing higher and higher within the lobbying group or on the staff of an executive agency/Congressional committee — all the while learning how best to manipulate the system toward whatever end he or she deems needed or those above have indicated they desire.

The people, of course, are again out of the picture. They haven't disappeared because they are still available to pay the taxes, fill out the forms and protest peacefully on cue; they are not there, however, to interfere with the policy that the lobbycrats have devised or question how it is to be carried out.

Revolving doors are more and more a part of government at all levels. The public is told it is getting a high paid executive with unquestioned experience in a technical area at a fraction of the cost that the private sector pays for such an individual; industry, we are told, accepts the loss of their valuable employee as a contribution to the common good. In reality, they get policy decisions that take the company's point of view seriously.

Look at how the revolving door works in practice :

- Dan Ashe served on the House Committee on Natural Resources from 1982 to 1995 and then went to work in the Clinton administration for the United States Fish and Wildlife Service — the agency that the same House committee deals with. Eventually Ashe was appointed director of the agency in 2011 and in that position oversaw a series of changes to regulations that he felt had no need for Congressiuonal review or approval.

- Linda Fisher served as Deputy Administrator of the Environmenal Protection Agency before working in the private sector as Chief Strategy Officer at DuPont and as an attorney at Monsanto — both frequent EPA targets.

- Philip Perry served as counsel to the 1996 US Senate hearings on campaign finance abuse. He later worked as a Bush-Cheney policy advisor and acting associate attorney general for the Department of Justice before moving to the Office of Management and Budget as general counsel. There he supervised the issuance of federal regulations. In between his federal work, he became a partner at Latham & Watkins, specializing in litigation and regulatory issues involving clients such as Monsanto and Lockheed Martin. His experience and contacts in government did him no harm in serving their needs.

- Meredith Atwell Baker was appointed to an executive branch position at the National Telecommunications and Information Administration in 2004 before becoming a commissioner at the Federal Communications Commission. In 2011, four months after voting to support the merger of Comcast and NBCUniversal, Baker accepted a job with the merged firm as "senior vice president of governmental affairs." Is the public well-served by this kind of personnel movement?

The revolving door is alive and well at the state level as well. Take Governor Jerry Brown's office in Sacramento. His executive secretary at the time this book was drafted is Nancy McFadde. She is the former chief lobbyist for one of California's largest utility companies, Pacific Gas & Electric. McFadden went to work for PG&E after she first worked for Governor Brown in the 1970s. McFadden was given a bonus of more than $1 million by PG&E before she rejoined Jerry Brown's staff in 2011.

The issue in terms of lobbycratic governance is whether the handsome farewell payment or McFadden's personal holdings of more than $100,000 in PG&E stock — along with options to acquire more — influenced any policy decisions or advice impacting PG&E. Key among her duties would be vetting potential appointees to the Public Utility Commission, the agency charged with setting rates and regulating the company's activities.

A cynic might think that her relationship with PG&E would color her attitudes in favor of the company; a true believer would say that her experience with PG&E was valuable to the governor. The author would only note that when one lobbycratic point of view is dominant — because of access or financing — lobbyists working the other side of the issue have a much harder time making their point of view heard.

FINAL POINT ON LOBBYISTS

The amount of money lobbyists spend to influence the legislation and regulation that govern our lives is indicative of the enormous influence that big organizations, groups and institutions now wield. Lobbyists are now so important to the functioning of California's government that it has institutionalized their presence. In a little known action, California's legislature, craven as ever to the money that lobbyists can provide, have designated the east door of the capitol building as their exclusive entrance. No waiting for them. They have important work to perform to make legislators look good.

While tourists anxious to see the building and citizens seeking to meet with a legislator wait in a queue at a separate door in Sacramento's sometimes torridly hot weather, lobbyists now have an unimpeded way to get in quickly, ply their enormous influence in the cooling air conditioning, and get out without any inconvenience.

Welcome to another way democracy works in the 21st century.

5.
THE TRIUMPH OF
THE TECHNOCRATS

We start this part of the discussion of lobbycratic governance with an explanation of how we differentiate a *bureaucrat* from a *technocrat*. Although bureaucrats certainly inhabit the halls and cubicles of enterprises in the private sector, technocrats are almost always associated with government agencies. There is a good reason for that.

BUREAUCRATS

After a stint in the U.S. Army, I became a Foreign Service officer at the State Department in Washington. There, I discovered that the most successful bureaucrats are those individuals who spend the bulk of their time maneuvering to get in the *middle* — a place between those below who served the agencies as the hunters and gathers of paper, data and impressions and the tribal chiefs above who were expected to absorb the paper, use the data, and react to the impressions in making decisions.

The middle they sought so assiduously was safe ground — far from having to deal with people, facts and reality or the pressures, doubts and disappointments that come with deciding issues. Staying in the middle, I observed, is not easy. Among the hunters and gathers in the civil service are hordes of others who are also seeking to be comfortable and protected in the middle. No blame attaches to those in the middle for failing to do something or doing something wrong; it is a place where the individual is shielded from claims of venality and corruption that often attach to a decision, whether done honestly or gone bad. In a word, the middle is a quiet spot hidden from view between those who deal with reality and those who dispose of it.

Middle seekers are found *within* every level of a bureaucracy. Many exalted members at the top of the civil service are always looking for ways to pass the need for a decision laterally to someone else for collateral action, commentary or opinion, down to someone for more information or further investigation, or up the chain of command to someone at a higher pay grade. The middle seeker is the person that gives bureaucracies the reputation for not getting much done. Most don't. But that, or course, is the goal of so many involved in large, heavily compartmentalized organizations. Decisions attract attention and have consequences; decision-avoidance makes few ripples. The middle also offers endless space to be unaccountable for questionable and sometimes illegal conduct.

Bureaucracies may well have also been the first to identify Murphy's Law: Anything that can go wrong will go wrong. They were certainly among the first to deal with the consequences of Murphy's Law —

make sure that responsibility for what goes wrong attaches to someone else working somewhere else.

Hence, professional experienced bureaucrats learn that the middle provides a barrier from criticism and controversy as well as protection from danger and grunt work.

Perhaps the modern American military is the best place to understand a bureaucratic mentality. If an officer is always on time, enthusiastic and efficient at handling matters to and from people below his station and passing on matters in an orderly fashion to those above his station, he avoids anything negative. Those who have a clean record of always being on time, enthusiastic and efficient tend to be promoted while those who have some blemish on their record because they did something that strayed outside of the lines may not go as far.

In recent days those officers who have taken no risks, made no mistakes, followed the rules and kept out of trouble have lasted the longest. They are likely to be the ones that end up rewarded for their clear records and competent diligence with regular promotions. A lot of them end their careers with flag status. The problem is that sometimes individuals who float effortlessly to the top by creating no wake tend to lack the imagination, the flair and the experience in making tough decisions required to exercise effective leadership.

Of course, assertions like this, particularly about the military, always attract instant, vehement and continuous denials. How dare someone denigrate as "bureaucrats" our "heroes" — the men and women who put their lives on the line every day to protect everyone else's freedom? Simple. First of all, the term "bureaucrat" can be a neutral rather than a pejorative term. They are people who carry out policy but do not contribute to it or are not authorized to make a decision alter it. Secondly, as someone who served among them and saw first hand how far many in the military go to be out of danger for most of their careers — but rack up medals for place and process rather than for bravery — it is an observation that I am comfortable making if others are not.

TECHNOCRATS

Technocrats are bureaucrats as well. But they are a breed of American bureaucrat who *seek* ways to make their views and ideas heard; they want decision authority to move a process or program forward. Once committed to a point of view, they tend to resent interference. It happened in 2016 when a group of some 100 individuals in science and industry took a full page ad in *The New York Times* to protest a decision by some of the country's most powerful attorneys general to investigate their position on climate change. The ad called on "every American to reject the use of government power to harass or silence those who hold differing opinions [from those approved by the] government." Protest or not, intimidation is a favorite tactic of those involved in lobbycratic governance.

Sometimes, of course, technocrats are content to move decisions sideways — when even a technocrat seeks the safety of the middle. It can occur when a bureaucracy has an exposed problem — a failure to reassign a teacher accused of improper conduct, a bottleneck on a freeway caused by a decision to do maintenance at the start of a three-day holiday, or a bad guy who slipped through the cracks. Instantly, technocrats urge that the matter be reviewed, examined and dealt with internally within the agency. The politicians with responsibility for oversight hastily agree.

No outside eyes or prying interviews, thank you. Give no opening to some hotshot lawyer looking to make a name for himself or some radical interest group looking for additional contracts. Nope. Assign a few trusted equals from elsewhere to find the "understandable" explanation for the problem, offer a reasonable solution to assure the public it won't happen again, and hope the matter is soon overwhelmed by the next crisis or forgotten.

Technocrats also seek the middle when they suggest temporary solutions for major problems. Structural faults with bridges is just such a case in point. The cost of building new bridges and other elements of the country's crumbling infrastructure is a daunting prospect to both technocrat and politician. It requires multiple difficult choices involving design, direction, capacity, materials, costs and the like. The problem is that these decisions can have no immediate benefit to either the technocrat nor the politician. In fact, the bigger the project, the more disruption for longer periods of time, that makes for angry citizens.

When was the last time you thanked someone for the courage to cause immediate pain in the hope that it may result in major relief in the future? Right. Never. So technocrats and politicians alike tend to avoid long term solutions in favor of the easy way out — *the temporary fix*. This may exacerbate the problem in time, may add to overall costs, but it gets the matter off of their backs for the present. Best of all, the temporary fix can look like the technocrat and the politician handled the matter in a way that seems to solve the problem while allowing them to get out of Dodge City should the fix collapse around them.

If it does, who gets blamed? Not those who decided on the temporary fix. Who can identify the individuals who may have shirked their responsibilities? Worse, those in office at the time of a disaster — not those who failed to act when the problem might have been solved — catch the political heat. So why not pass the problem to the next person holding your current position as you climb the career ladder to new heights and look forward to a very comfortable and rewarding retirement, remembering all the good that you did and ignoring all the hurt that might have been avoided.

Technocrats also serve as the institutional memory of a public agency. They not only *know* how to keep the ship of state running smoothly by treating the past as prologue, but they have a penchant for wanting to be in control of the institutional process going forward. It has developed to the point that elected and appointed officials have become subservient to a vast army of permanent civil servants.

Take the case of former Secretary of State Hillary Clinton. As noted before, she was cited in May 2016 by the State Department's Inspector General for violating "departmental policy" when she failed to "seek permission" to establish her private email system. State's IG noted that had she sought the permission of departmental officials — the technocrats that nominally work *for* a Secretary of State — "it would not have been granted." Wow!

We are in an era when unnamed civil servants — the technocrats that occupy positions of responsibility within the State Department — determine policies that all employees must follow — including the Secretary of State. In another instance, the Secretary of Energy learned in the 1990s of Russian equipment that used small amounts of electricity to split air polluting molecules into their harmless components. She asked her technocrats in West Virginia to test the Russian's Pulsatech equipment. They did, but grumbled about not having been consulted in advance. To show their "value," they changed the test goals at the last moment without informing the Russians. Not surprisingly, the equipment failed to meet U.S. standards; the Secretary was dutifully informed. The technocrats won. But we will never know how much the public lost by not having the Russian equipment available to clear the air.

What has happened to the words richly printed on the commissions that Presidents sign?

Reposing special trust and confidence in your

Integrity, Prudence and Ability, I have nominated you by and with the advice and consent of the Senate, do appoint you [office name] and do authorize and empower you to hold said office and to execute and enjoy all of the rights, privileges and immunities thereunto appertaining during the pleasure of the President of the United States.

Appointees of the President may receive, frame and display these soaring words of authority on their ego walls, but they have lost their effective power. The technocrats have rendered them meaningless and the governing elite have accepted the situation. Many believe that when technocrats within a vast bureaucracy assume the power properly accorded by the concept of democracy to the people or their elected representatives, it is tantamount to the inmates taking over the asylum. It is just one more consequence of lobbycratic governance.

In other cultures, technocrats have other titles but filled essentially the same role they now serve in the United States. They were the scribes of the ancient civilizations, eunuchs famously serving the Chinese emperors, the Imperial Household advisors to the Emperors of Japan, the senior aristocrats that hovered close to the thrones of European monarchs, the cadres that served Communist governments, and the permanent secretaries of the ministries of parliamentary governments.[†]

[†]Interestingly, Mark Kurlansky in his meticulously researched 2016 book *Paper* reports that paper itself was developed to fill a need of early civil administrators — the technocrats of such civilizations as Sumeria— in order to communicate with outlying areas and record matters permanently.

Understanding more about each of these other types of technocrats provides insights into how our own operate. All of these officials from other cultures exemplify an old saying: *Those closest to the centers of power get power of their own*:

CHINA — The Chinese imperial court began using eunuchs as senior officials to the emperors during the Han Dynasty (206 BCE to 220 CE). Eunuchs were given power because of the belief that men unable to produce heirs would not covet political power or riches to pass on to *their* sons; they would pose no threat to the rulers of the day. Quaint thinking, but naive at best.

In managing the affairs of the palace, the eunuchs vied for power with military leaders, scholars and specialists in the various ministries. Because they wielded their power so closely to the emperor, they were universally viewed by outsiders as scheming and corrupt, often cast as villains in theatrical dramas. But rather than achieve their power from *technical* prowess, they got it mostly by raising male heirs in the palace in their own image. The eunuchs molded these boys to suit their own ambitions. Children who became emperors before reaching adulthood were taught to rely heavily on the wisdom of the family eunuchs and kept away from other government advisors during their formative years.

JAPAN — Technocratic power in Japan centered on the Imperial Household Ministry — a unit of government that has taken care of the emperor's family and Royal Palace matters since 701 CE. While the emperor himself was considered a living deity of the Shinto religion, his powers were often only symbolic. Bercauise hje was so isolated, few in the public knew that members of the Imperial Household Ministry assumed a license to run matters in the emperor's name. For the most part, the Ministry was run by the aristocrats of powerful families for the benefit of these families and their allies.

As if to prove the point, Emperor Meiji (1867-1912) was said to be an indulgent womanizer, difficult to get under control. As a result, great effort was made by the Household Ministry to train his heirs in order to make them compliant and dependent on the family's advisors. Emperor Hirohito, grandson of Meiji, was so closely connected to his councillors that it complicated Japanese decision-making during World War II. After the war, imperial power and financial independence was placed under the authority of the Japanese prime minister. A Household Ministry still exists, but it does not have any of the powers it once claimed.

CADRES — Technocrats in the Soviet Union and modern China are an integral part of the Communist Party. They are indoctrinated into the Party philosophy and trained to control government operations becoming the link between the country's small leadership group and the rest of the people in the country. Mao Tse-tung described the role of the cadres this way:

It is on these cadres . . . that the Party relies for its links with the membership and the masses, and it is by relying on their firm leadership of the masses that the Party can [defeat the enemy.]

The collapse of the Soviet Union in 1991 brought the return of Russia and changes in the other 15 nations that had comprised the U.S.S.R. In China, the Party is on unsteady grounds because of rampant corruption that developed among the cadres. They had been given so much autonomy that they began to ignore popular policies for programs of their own devising and for the benefit of their own families.

Journalist Jonathan Watts believes that the Chinese government itself is actually a technocracy, controlled by those at the top of the 80 million members of the Communist Party.

Many senior cadres — large numbers of whom are now the "princeling" sons and daughters of former leaders — use party connections for self-enrichment in an increasingly divided society.

ENGLAND — Technocratic power in England dates back to the reign of Elizabeth I. She was crowned in tumultuous times that forced her to rely heavily on her close advisors and courtiers. Elizabeth retained many councillors from her sister Mary's reign and several that had served on the Privy Council for her father, Henry VIII.

At the time, it was practically unthinkable to dismiss these long-serving aides from the monarch's staff; nearly all of them were aristocrats with extensive landholdings and political control of the population. The Privy Council had assumed immense power as advisors, administrators and planners for the Crown — "the eyes, the ears and the tongue of the Prince and the realm." That nicely sums up the power that technocrats everywhere still covet.

The pinnacle of modern day technocratic power is held in Britain today in the permanent secretaries at each government ministry. They are responsible for the day-to-day operations of their departments. Given the enormous power they wield and the tenuous control exercised by the political leadership that can change from election to election and often in between as well, it is surprising how opaque the appointment process of permanent secretaries remains. They are nearly always appointed from within an agency without any formal competition. It suggests that technocrats once in power do not relinquish it easily. No less a person than Prime Minister David Cameron had this to say in 2011 about what the government confronted in the way of technocratic power:

> . . . bureaucrats in government departments . . . concoct those ridiculous rules and regulations that make life impossible, particularly for small firms. [Henceforth, they are to] simplify the language they use in ministerial submissions and not hide bad news in complexities."

Have the technocrats heeded the command of the Prime Minister and made the regulations they promulgate easier and simpler for ordinary British citizens to follow? Nothing I have read in the last five years would suggest that the public is noticeably better off. That, of course, is one of the great strengths of the permanent civil service in any democratic society. The political leadership of the agencies of government come and go, particularly in parliamentary regimes that have no fixed term of office. That made the signal to the British fleet in 1939 that "Winston is back" particularly unusual. It heralded the return of Winston Churchill to the Brititsh cabinet as First Lord of the Admiralty after leaving that position "in pain and sorrow almost exactly a quarter of a century before." He was that rare cabinet minister who used his position to accomplish real change.

THE GROWTH OF TECHNOCRACY

In the United States, the technocrats are equally well-entrenched and growing in their control of government. While the politicians have been their usual acquiescent selves and the rest of us have been paying our usual no mind to the business of government, the technocrats have been on the move. Look at these figures on government pay:

> In 2008, the Department of Transportation had only one employee earning $170,000 per year; by 2015, 1,690 employees were earning at least that much. The Defense Department had 1,868 employees earning more than $150,000 in 2008; in 2015, that number had ballooned to 10,100!

Government employees, as a group, are one of the most powerful special interests in Washington.

While they don't react uniformly to every issue, they can unite around such matters as wage maintenance, employment benefits and government privileges to obtain what they want.

For example, nearly every museum and zoo in America charges an admission fee. Citizens who support these facilities with their taxes are okay with this. Why then are all of these facilities totally free in Washington? We know the ritualistic claim that Washington is every American's second home town so its facilities ought to be open and welcoming when they are visiting. Generous thought, but it would also be nice if the people who live in the capital city didn't ask the rest of us to also comp them and their neighbors into the same facilities for free. Why not do what many foreign governments do, but a little differently: Allow visitors to enter for free while charging those who live in the surrounding area a nominal entrance fee.

This would not be much of a burden given the fact that the average government employee *costs* taxpayers $123,049 in 2009 while the average cost of a private sector employee in the same year was $61,051. In short, Washington's civil servants and those who deal with them can afford the price of admission.

There is another hometown phenomenon that makes Washington unique. While the rest of the country was stressing in the spring of 2016 over long security lines at airports around the country — causing as many as 40 percent of American Airlines passengers to miss their flights — no such problem was reported at airports in Washington, D.C. Not surprising.

No technocrat at headquarters wants to hear personally from someone in a higher pay grade that they, their colleagues or their families missed a flight or had to arrive at Dulles International or Reagan National three hours before a flight — as was recommended elsewhere in the country; none of them wanted to read in the *Washington Post* that their agency was causing the problem. So as is typical for lobbycratic governance, the technocrats took care of themselves first. Extra personnel were brought in, overtime was authorized, leaves were cancelled and the problem was avoided in Washington. The rest of the country? Not so much.

The power to make things happen that also happen to benefit one's own interests is heady stuff. When I was a second lieutenant in the Army, I was given responsibility for preparing the annual budget to cover the costs of running and maintaining a small military post on New Jersey's Sandy Hook peninsula. All the other officers on the staff considered it a thankless task. But I relished the opportunity. Majors, colonels and even a general officer were asking me to provide money to resolve particular problems in their commands. I had the power to recommend shaving expenditures in various accounts here and there to be able to make the savings available to satisfy at least part of each commander's request. My colonel loved satisfying his colleagues; I loved the power that was far above my rank.

When I later entered the U.S. Foreign Service I asked to be given a budgetary position at a major embassy as my first assignment. The request was summarily refused. I was told that my background and experience destined me for a major *political* role in America's diplomatic corps — future Ambassadorial material. I needed to embellish those credentials from the start rather than be tainted as some kind of administrative specialist.

Happily the Under Secretary of State for Management learned of my special interest and pulled me into a program he was initiating at President Kennedy's behest. Kennedy had seen the need for better coordination of American interests in London, where his father once served as ambassador to the Court of St. James. He wanted better coordination of all non-State agencies for *his* appointees at U.S. embassies. Working to enhance ambassadorial power showed me the reality of how American foreign policy is actually crafted. It also brought me a special understanding of such diverse agencies as the CIA, Defense, FBI, the Foreign Agricultural Service, the IRS, Customs, the Smithsonian Institution and the Library of Congress.

It was this exposure to the culture and internal politics of so many agencies that I would later identify as part and parcel of how lobbycratic governance works.

6.
THE SUBSERVIENCE OF
THE POLITICIANS

With lobbyists and technocrats now doing the heavy lifting of developing government policies and devising the procedures to implement them, elected officials and high-level political appointees have drifted back to third place in the pantheon of players involved in the American scheme of governance. In fact, the public's view of politicians is sinking rapidly as reflected in this story now circulating on the Internet:

Some surgeons at a convention are discussing who makes the best patients. The first offers this thought: "I like to work on accountants because when you open them up, everything is numbered." A second likes electricians. "Everything inside of them is color coded." A third surgeon from Washington, D.C. says: "Politicians are the easiest to operate on. They have no guts, no heart, no balls, no brains, and no spine. Plus the head and the ass are interchangeable."

This view might seem a touch brutal to some, right on the mark to others. Oddly, to members of the media and political staffers it may be shocking. They tend to treat politicians as if their views really count. For the most part, though, they don't. In fact, members of the U.S. Congress have a strange profile — accepted or appreciated individually by their constituents and reviled collectively as part of a legislative body.

- As a result, nearly all members of Congress are continually reelected from their districts bi-year after bi-year;
- To reinforce the dichotomy, this bit of doggerel suggests the low esteem to which the Congress as a whole is held:

If *con* is the opposite of *pro*, is <u>Con</u>gress the opposite of <u>pro</u>gress?

Here may be one reason. An observer noted on an April 2016 *60 Minutes* broadcast that new members of Congress are told by their party leadership that their first (!) duty is to raise $18,000 a day — every day — to fund their reelection campaign. With such a mind set, it is not hard to see why a CNN exit poll, conducted among New Hampshire Republican primary voters on February 8, 2016, found that 47 percent "felt betrayed by Republican politicians."

Given the fact that most politicians are not spending much time legislating — the 114th Congress produced about half of the total number of bills in its first year of the average for the previous 20 Congresses — they have a lot of time to go on camera, to hone a quip, construct a quote, tweet a thought, post a comment, or lend an air of authority to their pronouncements. As one wag one put it, politicians measure their contributions in terms of "hoarsepower."

Despite the fact that the media gives them a lot of studio time and column inches as if they are important participants in the way the government conducts its business, they aren't. Reporters accord politicians disproportionate attention because of the titles they hold — quoting a Congressman makes it look like they have done their jobs when they get a pithy comment. But the reality is that between 85 to 92 percent of the American people — depending on the public opinion poll or when the interviews were conducted — believe that Congress, as an institution, has failed to meet its responsibilities. Polls asking the same question of state legislatures yield similar results.

DIVERSION/RECOGNITION POLITICS

One reason for the low esteem in which many elected legislators are held is their habit of engaging in meaningless activity and justifying it as substantive governance.[†] A case in point is all the

---

[†]If not engaged in meaningless politics, politicians can become infamous for what they don't do. One example, among dozens, is the fact that Michigan and Mississippi remain the only states that still consider unmarried cohabitation a crime, even in the face of Florida's decision "that

huffing and puffing in Washington over whether calling its professional football team the "Redskins" is actually *degrading* to Native Americans or just a way of keeping Indian issues in the news. Boycotts are another noisemaking, but relatively punchless strategy, to give the impression of doing something without causing much hardship on either side.

But in the politics of diversion, nothing beats sponsoring a resolution to declare a particular day or week in honor of some individual, industry or group. We have all smiled when a news summary on the radio or a final piece on a television news broadcast reminds us that this is [FILL IN THE DATE], so it must be —

February 15	Susan B. Anthony Day
March 25	Greek Independence Day
May 22	National Maritime Day
September 11	Emergency Number Day
September 28	National Good Neighbor Day
October 6	German-American Day
October 15	White Cane Safety Day
November 15	America Recycles Day
December 17	Wright Brothers Day

These may strike many as silly — especially when legislators have designated May 1 as Loyalty Day

living in sin" seemed oddly none of the state's business in 2016. When politicians hide behind recognition politics and social engineering, it opens the door for lobbyists and technocrats to take control of the real business of government.

and September 11 as Patriots Day without bothering to explain the difference. Legislators have also fallen all over themselves to give their constituents with retail businesses, entertainment facilities and restaurants National Child's Day [first Monday in June], Parents Day [last Sunday in July] and Grandparents Day [first Sunday after Labor Day] to match the nearly universally recognized Mother's Day [second Sunday in May] and Father's Day [third Sunday in June] with the apostrophe in tact. But in an era where politicians are fulfilling concierge roles — and getting consistently re-elected for these kinds of activities — all of this makes sense.

MOCKING POLITICIANS

It also makes sense to anyone trying to sort out what American politicians actually do in the 21st century. Take a 2016 *Doonesbury* cartoon by Garry Trudeau. The six panels depict someone watching what appears to be a Sunday political talk show on television. In the first panel, the host of the show makes a statement:

> . . . .*rising sea levels are now regularly inundating South Florida and creating small ponds in the streets, many with swimming fish, with a million-plus septic tanks at risk of failing, local leaders are scrambling to cope . . . and yet you remain a climate change denier.*

The TV talk sow host then asks Senator Rubio, the Florida senator running at the time for the Republican nomination for President but never portrayed in the strip, the following question:

Why is that?

Senator Rubio responds:

Because I'm not a scientist. I'm a leader for the 21st century.

The show host suggests:

But if nothing is done, almost $70 billion worth of property could be flooded by 2030.

Rubio responds:

Again, I'm a leader for the 21st century. I am not a claims adjuster.

The show host persists:

But you represent Florida . . .

The senator corrects that statement with this comment:

No, I represent a new generation of leadership for the 21st century.

Finally, the host makes one last try at connecting the perceived problem to a perceived problem solver:

Okay, but didn't the 21st century start 15 years ago?

Only to get this reaction from Senator Rubio:

I'm not a mathematician.

Today, more and more politicians are equally shy about taking positions that may backfire on their electability in years to come. Moreover, those who fail to take an identifiable position on any issue are less likely to be vulnerable to future political attacks.

At the same time that Garry Trudeau was mocking Senator Rubio's Presidential aspirations, other cartoonists were having fun with North Carolina's legislature. It voted in 2016 to stop individuals from using public bathrooms that do not correspond to their sex at birth. One cartoonist wondered how the law might be enforced and drew a guard posted in front of a ladies' room armed with a microscope and flashlight and surrounded by signs requiring a birth certificate and a photo I.D. Another cartoonist drew a legislator offering another law called the bathroom transparency act. It would mandate that every stall in every bathroom be equipped with a glass door.

But no matter how absurd the law in North Carolina struck some — and discriminatory to others — it was a major win for organizations representing the conservative right and a loss for groups representing the lesbian, bisexual, gay, transgender and questioning communities. Such a result is virtually inevitable in a polarized society. No sooner had the bill passed by large majorities in Raleigh than an organization representing the affronted side filed a federal lawsuit to overturn the new law. Soon thereafter, a federal executive order mandated that all school facilities were required to allow anyone to use a bathroom that matches the gender identity they have chosen.

Some legislators have avoided making awkward decisions. One in California was notorious for never voting yea or nay on any issue; he voted present and thought himself brilliant in how he avoided making enemies. Other have retreated by joining one of the many "caucuses" that have now formed, notably in the U.S. House of Representatives. The Congressional Black Caucus is one of the most famous. But did you know that there is also a Congressional Czech Caucus and an American Sikh Congressional Caucus? If not a member of a particular caucus, Representatives can avoid establishing a personal position by joining a "coalition," "study group," "working group, or "task force." Many other countries use the term "parliamentary group" to achieve the same purpose.

By their nature caucuses establish a point of view on a topic, allows members of the legislature to telegraph to their constituents and funding sources fidelity to a particular broad concern, but allows them to skip votes, avoid hard thought, make few verbal gaffs and otherwise stay out of trouble on vexing details that may conflict with a district's needs. The largest of these caucuses are the political parties themselves — known as the House Democratic Caucus, the House Republican Conference, the Senate Democratic Caucus, and the Senate Republican Conference. It is these groups that do the "deciding" on major issues.

Because these caucuses are often divisive and therefore indecisive, a new non-partisan problem-solver caucus has formed, sponsored by a good government vehicle created by former Senator Joe Leiberman and former Governor Jon Huntsman. The Problem Solver Caucus is designed to demonstrate the interest of caucus members in finding ways to cooperate rather than to be in continual conflict. By mid-2016, the caucus was said to comprise some 80 members.

VOTING FOR DOLLARS

Many politicians today decide, with the help and analysis of their party caucuses and their personal staffs, how to cast a vote on the basis of which side will personally do them the most good. How is that determined? Politicians count potential voters in the next election — and the number of voters to be counted on is dependent on the flow of money. It keeps voters aware of their successes. It keeps them traveling, making speeches. Supporting the position of an organization generally translates into direct contributions by the organization's lobbyists and principal members to a politician's campaign funds or results in a major donation to a political action group supporting the politician.

Sometimes, it is not the money but the in-kind donations that make a difference. One candidate in Los Angeles, seeking to switch from City Council to a much more powerful position on the County Board of Supervisors, saw 50 billboards go up supporting the change. He said he had nothing to do with the billboard firm's decision. That's no doubt true. But he is a member of the city's Land Use Management Committee, which has jurisdiction over the company's application to convert dozens of its billboards to a digital format. Is this corrupt or just business as usual in a government where politicians are beholden to lobbying interests? Interestingly, the councilman lost his race, but the billboard company still looks to benefit from its generosity.

Money, in fact, dominates the time and attention of most candidates and elected officials today. Both parties have calling centers adjacent to the Capitol where officials go on a regular basis to dial for dollars. John Oliver on HBO's *Last Week Tonight* reported that candidates for the House and Senate raised a staggering $1.7 billion in 2014 for their campaigns. Most office holders spend a lot of their of their time on the task of raising funds. Most staffs are said to reserve four hours a day, each day, for their principals to be on the phone asking for contributions. One Congresswoman was recorded as calling a lobbyist to tell him that she had noticed that his organization had not yet contributed to her re-election campaign. She suggested that $3,000 would prevent any bad thoughts from settling in. It's blatant, perhaps, but effective at refilling a campaign war chest.

When they are not on the phone, politicians are hosting a fund raising function. The Sunlight Foundation counted 2,800 such functions in Washington, D.C. in 2014. With only about 340 days a year available for such events — federal holidays linked to 3-day weekends louse up the calendar — catered events were literally being held morning, noon and night. The Half Shell restaurant on Capitol Hill — a quick and convenient in and out for both politicians and lobbyists — was said to have booked *948* functions that year. When you think of who in Washington has the time and money it takes to attend these events, it is not hard to figure that lobbyists collect a drawerful of name tags in even-numbered years.

When outside of the capital, candidates and office holders are working their wealthy contacts for donations. Listen to how Peggy Noonan used a 2016 column to describe the five -figure-per-head cocktail parties and dinners that unfold in New York:

> *Candidates for president only come to [the city] for major media interviews and for money. They pick Manhattan up and shake it like a big pink piggy bank — 60K at the downtown breakfast, $600K at the uptown cocktail party. They enter the homes of the great and powerful — the spacious rooms, high ceilings, plump sofas, shiny floors, important art, views of Central Park —and they think: "Boy, they sure got it good. Maybe the economy isn't so bad!" The rich of New York thus hold an outsized place in the Republican and Democratic imagination. But the not-rich — the middle, the hanging-on and the poor — have no place at all. Republicans especially . . . have no sense of them. They know the hedge-funders and the rooms with the Rothkos. Their vision [of everything else] comes from old movies like "Dog Day Afternoon."*

Some of the people providing the funds for politicians deal directly with office holders and candidates; they don't mess with breakfasts, cocktails, dinners or other fancy functions. Charles and David Koch, the enormously wealthy and politically active brothers, spend their money promoting their mostly conservative political agenda through friendly organizations and specific politicians. Charles Koch gave a rare television interview in 2016 to Kai Ryssal of *Marketplace*. That sparked the following fable written for *The New*

Yorker's website by humorist Andy Borowitz:

Koch Brothers Consider Purchasing First Democrat

Charles and David Koch, the billionaire industrialists who have spent decades acquiring a world-class collection of Republicans, revealed over the weekend that they are considering purchasing their first Democrat.

"We've always bought Republicans, and our father bought Republicans before us," Charles, the elder Koch, said. "They're bred to be obedient, and they respond to simple commands."

Koch said that he and his brother learned, after making some phone calls, that other oligarchs have bought Democrats in the past, and "had good experiences with them."

While acknowledging the risk inherent in owning their first Democrat, Koch said that it would probably turn out to be a better investment than some of the Republicans they have recently purchased.

The fascinating aspect of political humor is that there are always a germ of truth to be found behind the specific words.

POLITICAL HARDBALL

In lieu of or in addition to the money they provide politicians, some special interest organizations can produce an army of warm bodies to participate in a politician's campaign in return for support for an issue of importance to the organization. Sometimes the lobbying organization takes charge of an issue and essentially carries the politicians along for the ride.

Such was the case in California in 2016 when a big union showed its political muscle by pushing for passage of legislation while threatening to sponsor a tougher proposition on the November ballor. Members of the legislature may be lazy and self indulgent, but they aren't stupid. They approved a a more business friendly path to a higher minimum wage..

The bill passed by the legislature and signed by the governor increases the minimum wage by $1 per hour each year until it reaches $15 per hour in 2020.. The Service Employees International Union didn't hide its role in organizing the legislative vote or in orchestrating public awareness of the issue. With 700,000 members paying dues of around $58 per month, the available political funds and the amount of voter interest it can generate through extended families and their friends can be substantial.

Opposing lobbying groups were overwhelmed by the SEIU onslaught. All in all, it provided an unambiguous look at how lobbycratic government works at the state level. But while the raw power of big unions with big money was on display, the politicians publicly sung each other's praises about all the hard work they did to make the minimum wage bill a reality. They didn't do much as far as we could tell, but the media nevertheless gave the politicians great credit for merely gong along.

The problem is that an element of the public doesn't see the duplicity involved and clings to the belief that their elected representatives actually take the views of citizens into account in the halls of government. Unfortunately, the truth is that they don't.

It doesn't matter whether organizations provide money or bodies. Both are about equal in determining the politicians' career prospects. Unless a lobbyist represents something BIG, it is unlikely he will make much of a dent in the political process. The message today is that unless you are among the BIGS, you are really not competitive. Nice that you want to participate, but don't expect too much in response from a politician.

PERKS OF OFFICE

Politicians reward themselves handsomely for the services they perform. A California legislator earns $100,113 per year plus $168 a day while the legislature is in session,[†] plus a pension to see them through retirement. Some even earn more than one public pension: John Moorlach gets $83,800 per year for having been Treasurer of Orange County and still more as a former County Supervisor; Assemblyman Jean Cooper receives $112,980 for his days as a Sheriff's captain and a big salary besides.

[†]Karen Bass, a California congresswoman, first ran for her Westside Los Angeles House seat in 2010 as "Speaker of the Assembly Emeritus." That little bit of pomposity — California is awash with speakers emeritus in an era of term limits — was matched by her pretending to be doing the people's business in Sacramento while she was campaigning on a daily basis in Los Angeles, unabashedly collecting her $168 extra per day. And how did voters react to her little cheat? They nominated her with 85 percent of the vote. As Shakespeare said, the fault "is not in our stars . . . but in ourselves." Or as Pogo once proclaimed: "We have met the enemy and he is us!" Exactly. Only voters can end lobbycratic governance. Perhaps they will when they finally get fed up with how politics rare practiced today in Washington and the state capitals.

Then there are the perks of office. Many of these perks are provided by lobbyists or their organizations and are not designed to influence an elected or appointed official on a *specific* piece of legislation. Rather, they are meant to establish a mood and favorable attitude for the long term. California legislators reported receiving tickets to see the LA Dodger in the World Series and the Golden State Warriors in the NBA championships; being treated to golf course green fees and free flights on private aircraft there and back from law firms, consulting groups, and others with political business in Sacramento. Would any of these extras influence how the members of the legislature react to issues of interest to their benefactors? Of course not!

Here is an example of why small guys really don't have a realistic chance in the era of lobbycratic governance. The president pro tem of the California State Senate at the time this book went to press is Kevin de Leon, a Democrat from Los Angeles. Late in 2015, he ginned up a trip to Australia to "look for drought solutions" applicable to California. After he returned, we never learned whether he found any. His spokesperson put the best possible gloss on how come it took $14,055 to get to and back from Australia:

> As elected representatives of the world's seventh-largest economy and a gateway to international trade corridors, building global relationships and studying best practices in other countries is an essential part of the job description.

Ever recall hearing that blah, blah, blah before?

It's the kind of rhetoric flacks are paid to write and newspapers print because it comes from high office. The spokesman expanded the trip's purpose from the drought to make it a self-serving philosophy. Then to add to the *chutzpah,* she went on to say that the funding was provided by "respected non-profits." (A "respected" non-profit is political speak for another special interest group but also serves as a euphemism meant to convey "above board," "trustworthy" and "serious.")

The clincher in this standard rationale for justifying the perks of office is the signal to the public how concerned the politician is for his constituents: "Not a single taxpayer dollar" was spent on the trip, the media person added. Hooray. Don't you feel richer already? Of course, that "respected non-profit" paying to get Senator DeLeon to Australia and back was something called the California Foundation on the Environment and the Economy. Sounds righteous. But it is really just another smokescreen to hide actuality. The CFEE is funded by some notable BIGS:

- Pacific Gas & Electric Company
- Shell Oil
- Building and Construction Trades Council
- Chevron.

Is there any wonder that small groups feel helpless in trying to influence the way the legislature acts when they realize the capabilities of BIG organizations, BIG corporations and BIG labor unions to buy the attention of politicians? If you can provide a nice trip to the equivalent of Australia during legislative slow times, you, too, can become best friends with the president pro tem of the California Senate. He in turn controls the legislative agenda and future electability of at least half the other 39 senators in his chamber. It looks like a good investment if you have the kind of funds needed.

PG&E, Shell Oil, Chevron and the Construction Trades Council have those kinds of funds (and a lot more for that matter). They learned the technique of the overseas trip from one Milton Gordon, a former treasurer of the State of California. After leaving office, he dedicated himself to furthering the interests of Israel. Gordon organized annual all-expenses-paid 10-day trips to Israel for members of the legislature and their senior staff under the sponsorship of a major Jewish group in the U.S. and with the cooperation of the Israeli government.

Gordon's trips traditionally occurred in the dead zone between Veteran's Day and Thanksgiving — a notoriously quiet time for California government. Gordon concentrated on Gentile legislators or their important staffers. They always flew on El Al for security reasons, always stayed at the King David Hotel in Jerusalem, and were always exposed to both city life in Tel Aviv and kibbutz life in the desert. They saw all the important historic sites, visited all the important museums, saw all the sacred sites of the world's three Abrahamic religions.

In between they met with counterparts in the Israeli government, were received by the Prime Minister or another high-ranking official, and left feeling proud, knowledgeable and impressed. They became fierce defenders of Israel's interests and point of view thereafter — wherever in public life they found themselves.

The significance of Milton Gordon's operation was that when it comes to influencing government, a long view counts. Israel and its supporters were investing in the political class of a state with a large and influential Jewish population on the certainty that many of those who were invited on one of the annual trips to Israel would advance to higher office, perhaps to Washington, perhaps to a point of power that Israel could rely on. The donations of the BIGS to the California Foundation on the Environment and the Economy are likewise investments in maintaining their influence for long into the future. It's g'day mate for years to come.

Most of the BIGS involved in lobbycratic governance have the same vision. It is one of the reasons they are so strong and not easily defeated. They are on the battlefield for the long term; most individuals, most minor players, and most single-issue lobbying groups are not. They are famously one and done, goodbye — we are citizen/soldiers with other things to do. When you wonder how lobbyists got to be so strong and when you consider how difficult it will be to get the government back from their control, remember that politics is a marathon, not a mile.

Is there a countervailing force to the power that the BIGS can shower over the politicians? Of course. The people are the biggest interest group of them all. They can recover control of the government and take charge of creating the solutions if they wake up to the problem and become involved. But they have to be willing to pay attention, to do the hard work of actually taking back control of government and of continuing a consistent level of vigilance into the future. The penultimate chapter of this book gives specific ideas on how all of this can be done.

POLITICS AS A CAREER

James Roosevelt, the son of the former President and a Congressman from Los Angeles, used to say that being a member of Congress was a 20-year career. You had to be willing to put that kind of time into a House career to achieve any semblance of power in that body. He was not willing to wait. He was more in a hurry to earn substantial sums of money if he could not get to the political places that his father had been.

It was one of the reasons he shocked his supporters by suddenly resigning from his safe seat in the House of Representatives in 1965 — after five terms — and accepted Lyndon Johnson's appointment as U.S. Ambassador to the International Labor Organization in Geneva. It wasn't much of a diplomatic assignment, but it offered a platform to talk on labor issues that Congress had ignored.

The career aspect of politics — and the technocratic origins of many modern politicians — is no better illustrated by the rise of Asian Americans to elected office. Take the case of the Korean community in Los Angeles. Steve Kim was working in a downtown flower shop when the riots protesting the 1992 Rodney King verdict ravaged Koreatown.

Several months later a customer arranged to have Kim meet the new mayor's chief of staff. Wham. Bam. At age 25, Kim became Mayor Richard Riordan's liaison to the Los Angeles Korean community — just one of only two ethnic Koreans in City Hall

But it quickly became a fad. Every elected official needed a Korean-American staffer who spoke the language and could guide their fellow hyphenates through the maze of government procedures. Now, 25 years later there is an Asian Pacific American Legislative Staff Network — welcome to lobbycratic governance at the local level — and many of them are rising in elected offices:

> **David Ryu** began working as a staff member for Los Angeles County Supervisor Yvonne Brathwaite Burke. He is now an elected city councilman in Los Angeles.
>
> **John Chiang** was on Senator Barbara Boxer's staff. He was the California's controller for eight years, is now the elected state treasurer, and may run for Governor
>
> **Young Kim** is an elected Republican assemblywoman. She learned politics and made key financial contacts over a two decade career working for Congressman Ed Royce. He is now the Chairman of the House Foreign Relations Committee and she is on the way up in Sacramento.

While Koreans are on an electoral path in politics, others see the reality of politics as Jimmy Roosevelt saw them — choosing lobbying as the fastest road to a lucrative and influential future. Given the strength of lobbycratic governance, it won't be long before we are reading thatt Korean American lobbying groups are a more effective way to help the community than electing fellow ethnics to public office.

EXECUTIVE BRANCH

Politicians serve in the U.S. government in all three branches, although those in the judicial branch are getting thin on the ground. While common to the Supreme Court in its earlier days — think Chief Justices John Marshall, William Howard Taft and Charles Evans Hughes — jurists with significant political experience have not come to the Court since the days of William O. Douglas, Earl Warren and Sandra Day O'Connor. Nearly all Supreme Court appointees today come with heavy judicial experience that provides a long paper trail of written opinions to gauge their probable reactions to touchstone social and economic issues in the future. That's a shame. We could do with more jurists who have earned a living and been driven, in part, by responding to actual voter concerns.

Executive branch politicians are both elected — the President and Vice President — and appointed: Think the cabinet, subcabinet and some 1,200 other politically sensitive jobs. Think also about the White House staff and the bureaucracies within the Office of the President such as the National Security Council, the Council of Economic Advisers, and the Office of Management and Budget. Each of these agencies attracts ambitious political operatives.

The executive branch also includes all the cabinet

departments. It used to be that many of these departments were run by individuals with important political and electoral experience. Take Jack Kennedy's original cabinet in 1960, for example:

- Stewart Udall, an Arizona congressman, was appointed as Secretary of Interior;

- Orville Freeman left the governorship of Minnesota to become Secretary of Agriculture;

- Luther Hodges at Commerce had been governor of North Carolina; and

- Abe Ribbicoff was a senator and governor from Connecticut before assuming the position of Secretary of the Department of Health and Human Services.

And even when a scholar and technocrat like Dean Rusk — history professor, college dean, head of the Rockefeller Foundation — was selected by President Kennedy as his Secretary of State, the Kennedy team made sure that his assistant secretaries were experienced politicians such as New York Governor Averell Harriman (Assistant Secretary for Far Eastern Affairs), Michigan Governor G. Mennen (Soapy) Williams (Assistant Secretary for African Affairs), Fred Dutton, former Executive Secretary to California's Governor Pat Brown (Assistant Secretary for Congressional Affairs) and Illinois Governor Adlai Stevenson (Ambassador to the United Nations.)

Each of the old line cabinet departments — State, Justice, Treasury, Defense (as successor to the War and Navy Departments) — provides a political home for some fiercely independent and powerful bureaus with their own cultures:

- Internal Revenue Service in Treasury;
- Federal Bureau of Investigation in Justice; and
- the Foreign Service in State.

The newer cabinet departments such as Labor, Health and Human Services, Transportation and Homeland Security are collections of formerly fiercely independent agencies that had their own or other bureaucratic homes:

- The Bureau of Labor Statistics at Labor came out of the Commerce Department;
- The Social Security Administration was independent before becoming part of HHS;
- The Federal Aviation Agency was also an independent agency before Lyndon Johnson created the Department of Transportation; and
- The Coast Guard — long primarily a revenue arm of the government to ensure payment of customs duties (a major early source of federal revenue) — moved from Treasury to Transportation to its current place in Homeland Security. In time of war, however, the Coast Guard still. as always, reverts to the jurisdiction of the Defense Department.

Beyond the behemoth federal departments are the powerful independent agencies such as as the National Endowment for the Arts, the Environmental

Protection Agency, the Consumer Products Safety Commission, and a large number of independent regulatory agencies such as the Federal Communications Commission, the Federal Trade Commission, and the Security and Exchange Commission.

These regulatory agencies were originally formed because the details of controlling various aspects of American life became too onerous for Congress. In creating these quasi-executive, quasi-legislative agencies, Congress sought to professionalize the bureaucracy and relieve itself of work. The Interstate Commerce Commission was the first.

To get the railroads built across the continent, the government awarded the companies exclusive rights of way over federal lands that measured five miles on either side of the track to be laid. Once the railroads were running and commerce was being shipped along their routes, the railroads began to use their monopolies to charge whatever they wanted for the freight and passengers they carried. While other modes of transportation (wagons, barges) might still be available and convoluted routes using other railroads might be devised, the pain inflicted by BIG railroads on farmers, ranchers, trappers, and small businessmen became palpable.

When trying to set standards and rates became more than the Congress could do with any political comfort, the slow, inevitable and inexorable drift from a government trying to be of, by and for the people into one that we call —

LOBBYCRATIC GOVERNANCE

had begun.

One final point here: As the government became used to the work and output of the regulatory agencies, many of the same type of tasks were soon assumed by the executive departments as well. For example, the Fish and Wildlife Service within the Department of Interior added *regulation* of hunting and fishing activities to its original function of research, land management and wildlife protection. Later, when the U.S. signed the Convention on International Trade in Endangered Species of Wild Fauna and Flora (CITES), the Service assumed the management of an expanded American role in protecting elephants, rhinos, lions and other species in other lands.

More recently, the issue in many individual states focused on entrenched legislators — individuals elected time after time to the point that nothing was likely to dislodge them from office short of death, indictment or disability. Listen to the frustration incorporated into the California Constitution by the voters:

> *The people find and declare that the Founding Fathers established a system of representative government based upon free, fair, and competitive elections. The increased concentration of political power in the hands of incumbent representatives has made our electoral system less free, less competitive, and less representative.*

The pent up distrust of incumbent power got more specific in the subsequent paragraph that also remains embedded in the California Constitution:

> *The ability of legislators to serve unlimited number*

of terms, to establish their own retirement system, and to pay for staff and support services at state expense contribute heavily to the extremely high number of incumbents who are reelected. These unfair incumbent advantages discourage qualified candidates from seeking public office and create a class of career politicians, instead of the citizen representatives envisioned by the Founding Fathers. These career politicians become representatives of the bureaucracy, rather than of the people whom they are elected to represent.

The idea of term limits was approved by 52 percent of the electorate as Proposition 140 of 1990.

Subsequently 15 other states adopted similar restrictions. It was thought to offer a return to the era of citizen legislators, where people who knew what life was like in the real world served briefly in government before turning the responsibilities of office over to someone else. Talented and dedicated individuals would sacrifice a few years for public service and then return to their farms, ranches and private businesses to carry on with the lives they loved. And no one, of course, would catch the state capital equivalent of Potomac Fever. Wonderful. What a fantasy!

Term limits proved to have serious unanticipated consequences. First of all, no one wanted to go home to their farms, ranches and small businesses after being at the center of the action and the center of attention, especially with a high salary, paid staff and generous per diem account to boot. Rather than go home, most of the soon-to-be termed-out legislators began shopping for a new office to occupy.

Rather than new faces, term limits put the same faces in different offices. While another proposition was passed in 2006 to change the way term limits was working, it has never achieved its goal.

Secondly, instead of strengthening the bureaucracies, term limits *empowered* the lobbyists. They became the institutional memory and rules specialists for new members. And since no one ever wanted to appear as a prisoner of a staff inherited from a predecessor, legislators tended to turn to lobbyists for facts, opinions and perspective.

Hey, lobbyists. Welcome to the candy store.

FEDERAL BUREAUCRACY

While many of those we think of as politicians have never presented themselves as candidates for public office, elections are still the *sine qua non* of democratic governance. Before we look at all the ways that the political leadership has tried to change how elections are conducted, let's look at some statistics of governance in general.

According to a national survey conducted by the Pew Research Center in 2013, only a mere 19 percent of the respondents said that they trust the government in Washington to do what is right all or most of the time.

Given that many cabinet secretaries hold independent powers granted by Congress as well as a raft of powers delegated by the President, the fact that more than 80 percent of the people do not trust their government in one way or another is very disturbing. Yet the federal government employs some 2.7 million people and the same survey suggested that —

Sixty-two percent of respondents have a more favorable than unfavorable opinion of federal government employees.

The average citizen believes that the technocrats and bureaucrats do their jobs. That adds an important base of support for lobbycratic government.

ELECTIONS

While the bedrock of a democracy is often thought to be the right to chose freely among competing candidates to elect people to leadership positions, the entire concept of voting seems to be in doubt. Just as the American government no longer works in a traditional manner, the elections and the campaigns leading to them have changed as well. Today, for example, candidates put massive resources into opposition research to produce a detailed dossier of the other side's background, foibles and positions. It has become so effective as a campaign tool that the Republican Party now offers to contract out its staff for a fee to research and manage such private sector projects as proxy fights, annual meetings, public policy issues, competitive weaknesses, attack ads and the like.

Those with some years on the road well remember the dirty tricks of yore:

- The USC-trained Nixon operatives of 1968 raced across America, calling the local Democratic headquarters from a pay phone somewhere on the highway approaching a town.

As soon as the call was answered, the caller left the receiver dangling in place without saying a word. In that era, the line would stay open and prevent anyone in headquarters from receiving another call or calling out. Matters would remain that way until the phone where the call originated could be hung up.

- What about an Eisenhower-era trick of stuffing a paper clip under the lever of an electronic voting machine to prevent an electronic connection (vote) to record. An easier maneuver involved reversing the name identifications on each voting machine line. As a result, a vote for all Democratic candidates would actually register as a vote for all the Republicans involved in that election.

- My favorite trick, though, was the stunt that Dick Tuck pulled in the 1962 California gubernatorial race. Kids in the crowd were given signs to hold up welcoming Dick Nixon to Chinatown. While the English-language signs said "Nixon's The One," the signs in Chinese actually asked Nixon to explain the $200,000 loan that Howard Huges had made to his brother. When the press was tipped to the translation of the Chinese sign, it dominated the news story of the rally the next day and for many days thereafter.

- Every election season produces its own stories. In the 1856 Presidential race, for example, John Frémont supporters put out the rumor that the unusual tilt of James Buchanan's head — actually due to a congenital affliction — was the result of Buchanan's once trying to hang himself.

- In 1908, a Midwestern paper favoring William Jennings Bryan wrote this about his opponent, William Howard Taft, a Unitarian: "Think of the United States with a president who does not believe that Jesus Christ was the Son of God, but looks upon our immaculate Savior as common bastard and low, cunning imposter." Nice.

- In the 1950s, Jimmy Roosevelt's campaign manager scoured California's 26th Congressional District for a person with a similar name to Roosevelt's likely opponent. He found something close (the middle initial didn't match), qualified the bogus candidate for the ballot by gathering the required signatures and paying the necessary fees, and successfully confused voters with two guys with the same first and last name running for Congress. Which one was the "right" Republican? It didn't matter. Roosevelt was running in a safe Democratic district on the Westside of Los Angeles, but he, like Lyndon Johnson, ran for office as if every vote was in doubt until the polls closed.

- On the day of the Iowa caucuses in 2016, Senator Ted Cruz sent a tweet to all known Ben Carson supporters informing them that the retired neurosurgeon had decided to suspend his campaign. The implication was that with Dr. Carson out of the race, the supporters were free to caucus on behalf of Senator Cruz. The total fabrication, first reported on CNN but no doubt based on a rumor planted by a Cruz insider, may have helped Cruz win the most delegates in the Iowa caucuses that evening. Once exposed as the source of the rumor, the "TrusTED" banners that accompanied Senator Cruz at every campaign stop seemed to suggest that politics is still the same type of politics always practiced in American elections.[†]

- How afraid was the Republican party of facing Hillary Clinton in the 2016 general election? At least one party leader is reported to have urged Republicans in Nevada to register in both parties so they could vote *against* Hillary in a Democratic caucus. Since the state holds its party caucuses on separate days, it was actually possible to participate in both. One more strike against the sanctity of elections in a democratic society.

Beyond the schemes known as "dirty tricks" to those who suffer from them — innocent "pranks" to perpetrators — there are the real barriers that are put in place to discourage certain groups from voting.

- Some consider registration a barrier to vot-

[†]Ted Cruz campaigned hard thereafter, but was forced to suspend his campaign when he had no realistic way to win the Republican nomination after losing to Donald Trump in the Indiana primary. Trump became the nominee.

ing. Registration is designed to allow government authorities sufficient time to establish the various districts pertaining to a voters' residences. In most jurisdictions, all individuals can vote for a President, governor or mayor. But all other offices are determined by where the individual lives. Once eligible to vote, individuals are then required to cast a ballot in a certain place on a certain day between certain hours. Some jurisdictions make life easier for voters by permitting absentee or early voting.

- The push to make it harder for most people to vote began in 2010 when Republicans gained control of the majority of state legislatures. Democrats complained that the changes in voting laws were creating an older, whiter and more conservative electorate. As the demographics of the country change, laws that seem to punish younger voters and minority populations added to the ideological divide in the country. For example, Florida cut back on early voting; Ohio ended same day voter registration; New Jersey decided to stop online registrations. Restrictions on the time and place of voting are considered among the toughest barriers to overcome for those with jobs or workday family obligations.

- In some jurisdictions, educational barriers and identity requirements still act as barriers to voting. For example, in some states, being literate in English is a requirement for registering to vote. At least one state requires a prospective voter to be able to read the Preamble to the Constitution of the United States out loud to register. One voter in North Carolina said she spent 20 hours and travelled 200 miles to get a driver's license and voter registration documentation to have the proper information available on election day.

All of this leads us to question the very *validity* of elections themselves. What are they actually determining in an era of lobbycratic governance? Many elections can literally be bought, since *Citizens United* allows unlimited funds to be spent on behalf of a candidacy or cause. Most elections can be manipulated by a raft of dirty tricks expertly played on opposition campaigns. Are elections, as conducted in the United States today, as valuable a part of our form of government as common wisdom would have us believe?

While a further chapter looks in detail at ways that we might *change* our election procedures to make them better reflect the popular will, we could also consider how other democracies run their election procedures to see if any of these models would be workable in the United States.

- In some countries, voting is mandatory with fines assessed or citizenship privileges withdrawn for those who haven't voted.

- Los Angeles borrowed from a Latin American penchant to participate in lotteries to try to increase Hispanic participation. A private group offered a $25,000 prize to a voter chosen in a random drawing using ballot stub numbers. The concept was loudly ridiculed as the wrong way to increase voter participation for all the wrong reasons. After paying out the cash price, sponsors dropped the idea for any subsequent election.

- Many countries use proportional representation — elections where the number of seats are apportioned in the same percentage as the popular vote — to determine legislative seats. The U.S., for the most part, uses a winner take all approach in deciding winners.[†]

- In order to reduce outside influence on elections, many public bodies use the concept of electors — office holders who select others to service in offices of public trust. We do it in Presidential elections; the boards of directors of each Federal Reserve district nominates its president. Parliamentary systems select a prime minister by vote of all elected members; the public is not directly involved.

- Would some jurisdictions be better served if an elected body chose officials for offices that are currently filled by election — say those that now vote for sheriffs, assessors, treasurers, and judges? It is a question that is perpetually answered "yes" after years of

[†]The most important exceptions are Maine and Nebraska. They apportion their Presidential *electoral* votes by the percentage of the popular vote. Many political parties apportion the number of delegates to their national conventions according to the percentage of votes a candidate received in a state's primary election.

voters' being unable to distinguish one candidate from another in obscure nonpartisan races. It is always answered "no" when a political scandal erupts. Tom Hayden famously took control of zoning policy and density decisions in large areas by running his supporters for seats on local water boards. By denying water connections to developers, he stopped growth where he thought it harmful to a community.

The issue for some is whether these developments are bad for democracy *per se* or bad because they have become partisan issues that add to the ideological split between adherents on the fringes of both political parties. My response to its impact on democracy is that the U.S. does not own the definition of democracy and is not the only society capable of creating the standards for a democratic government. We make the mistake of assuming that what we do in the United States in terms of elections and democratic procedures are the world standard for such matters. They are not.

Do American barriers make it tougher to vote in the U.S. than elsewhere? Certainly. Does it matter? Probably not. The whole premise of this book is that the government is being run by lobbyists and technocrats under the watchful eye of lawyers with elected officials serving as their facilitators. So from this point of view, who *has* voted is not very crucial; who *will* vote in support of the changes advocated at the end of the book, is.

Campaigns for election in the United States have become stylized. For the most part, they follow similar paths because of reporting requirements and the election industry firms that do the strategy advice, issue research, opinion polling, event planning and media advertising.

Advertising in campaigns is not subject to fairness doctrines or disclosure rules. If the disclaimers accompanying pharmaceutical products and the listing of side effects seems overwhelming, political ads are just the opposite. Accuracy, honesty and completeness may be desired, but are hardly ever found. Californian political advertisers have been fooling voters with something called *slate mailers* for years. These are large postcards or small booklets published by official sounding groups that have nothing to do with either party. They are advertising vehicles selling space to any campaign willing to buy something that will be put in the mailbox of specific categories of voters in a certain ZIP code or electoral district. There are so many of them that they are clearly profitable; how effective they may be compared to other forms of advertising is another story. During the June 2016 California primary, we saw:

- The Coalition for California Newsletter. It endorsed 14 candidates — five Democrats, two Republicans and seven candidates for judgeships. The 8 by 5 1/2-inch four-page booklet was published by Voter News, which identified itself as a project of the Coalition for California. Sounded important.

- The California Senior Advocates League (CalSal) "endorsed" nine Republicans, one Democrat and six non-partisan candidates. CalSal's non-partisan endorsements matched those of the Coalition for California's slate mailer except for one candidate — clearly Ray Santana, a candidate for Superior Court judge, didn't pay to be in CalSal's piece and thus missed out on its "endorsement." He won his race nevertheless.

While giving the appearance of being sponsored by reputable, good government groups, slate mailers are purely business — big business at that and the public continues to buy into them as somehow a reputable organization that has made an honest judgment before endorsing one candidate or issue over another.

SCANDALS

One reason elected officials are held in such low esteem is the number of scandals that have unfolded in recent years. This does not necessarily mean that we have had more scandals of late than in earlier periods of American history. But with television and now the Internet, scandals become more immediate, more detailed and more sensational than newspapers and magazines were able to convey in earlier eras.

Most of the best remembered scandals seem to involve sexual matters rather than outright political cheating.

- The gold ring for recent sexual scandals is Bill Clinton's famous Oval Office liaisons with Monica Lewinsky. His attempts to deny the relationship and the evidence found on her blue dress eventually led to Articles of Impeachment being approved by the House of Representatives. While President Clinton was not convicted by the Senate of "high crimes and misdemeanors," the process pretty much ended the Clinton Administration's initiatives for the last two years of his second term.

- A few years later, Congressman Anthony Weiner — the husband of uber powerful Hillary Clinton aide and confidant Huma Abedin — was involved in *two* scandals related to sexting. The first time, he sent sexually explicit material via his cell phone to a woman in Seattle. The revelation of that bit of lack of judgment forced his resignation from Congress. The second incident of sexting occurred during his political "comeback" when he was campaigning for mayor of New York City. Despite the publication of explicit pictures from the second incident in July 2013, he refused to end his quest and ended up receiving just 4.9 percent of the final vote.

- The longest-serving Republican Speaker of the House of Representatives, Dennis Hastert, pleaded guilty to structuring a $1 million payoff for sexual abuse that occurred long before he was elected to Congress. He gave the million dollars in dribbles to a former student to keep him quiet about an abusive relationship Hastert had forced on the kid while a teacher and wrestling coach. But anti-drug laws require banks to report all cash withdrawals of more than $10,000 — ironically something that Hastert had supported. Hastert withdrew sums just under the threshold — an act that is also illegal if someone is trying to conceal a larger cash payment. Hence his pleas of guilty to a crime.

Hastert had been able to accumulate the amount of hush money involved from his work as a lobbyist. He had resigned his House seat in 2007, after the Democrats had regained the majority, to represent candy-flavored tobacco products and electronic cigarette interests in the corridors of Congress and the halls of the executive branch. He became part of the flotsam flowing through and around the revolving door that supplies most of the personnel of influence in lobbycratic governance.

- Former Oregon Republican Bob Packwood resigned from the Senate in 1995 after several years of allegations of sexual harassment from women — eventually numbering 19 — who had served on his staff.

- Martha Johnson, the head of the General Services Administration, was forced to resign in 2012 after a training session she authorized in Las Vegas was revealed to have cost taxpayers $820,000.

- As a result, nearly all members of Congress

- Representative Aaron Schock, a Republican from Illinois, resigned his Congressional seat in 2015 for using taxpayer money to pay for private jets, concert tickets, entertainment, photographers and most notably redecorating his office to look like the British manor house portrayed in *Downton Abbey*. That last bit of conceit is said to have cost taxpayers $40,000.

CORRUPTION

Money-oriented corruption seems so much tamer when viewed in light of sexual misconduct. After all, no less an authority than Henry Kissinger called political power the ultimate aphrodisiac. That noted, it is not surprising that corruption is the other inevitable downside of lobbycratic governance.

Corruption in the United States is not always of the unremorseful Mexican variety: *el que no transa, no avanza* — "if you don't cheat, you don't get ahead." Sometimes its just venal as in the case of Spiro Agnew — blatant, undisguised naked payoffs in return for government contracts.[†] They, of

---

[†]Recall that Richard Nixon's twice elected Vice President was forced to resign in 1973 when it became known that Spiro Agnew had received regular sums of cash from Maryland contractors for political favors done during the time he was Baltimore County's chief executive, Maryland governor, and Vice President of the United States. Agnew was succeeded by Gerald Ford, who became President when Nixon resigned under the procedures of the 23rd Amendment to the U.S. Constitution.

course, still exist as these more recent examples demonstrate:

- Representative James Traficant, a Democrat, was found guilty and expelled from office in 2002 for taking bribes from local businessmen, underreporting his income for tax purposes, and requiring his congressional aides to work on his farm.

- Dan Rostenkowski, another Democrat, was chairman of the powerful House Ways and Means Committee when he pled guilty in 1994 for corruption involving defrauding the government of more than $500,000. Charges included keeping "ghost" employees on his payroll, using congressional funds to buy gifts, using taxpayer money to pay for personal transportation, tampering with a grand jury witness, and exchanginig officially purchased stamps for cash. He served 17 months in prison for his crimes.

There is no doubt that corruption in the political sphere gives at least tacit permission to cheating among ordinary people. While we are prone to cluck our tongues in disgust whenever we hear of corruption in high places, we need to determine if that behavior has given license to cheating among the rest of us.

When we tolerate or condone any form of corruption in our own lives — as harmless or inconsequential as it may seem — it becomes very hard to demand a higher standard from the country's political leadership. And when there is tolerance for corruption at both ends of the political system, it becomes very hard to root out.

Just consider the amount of corruption that occurs outside the corridors of political power in this country. The U.S. endures considerable corruption everyday in the form of cheating that gives one person an advantage over someone else. Note this partial list:

> **Justifying a personal expenditure as a business expense on an expense report; providing home office needs from the company supply cabinet; claiming veterinarian bills as a family *medical* expense; tossing a substantial amount of trash into a dumpster someone else has rented; using uncancelled postage stamps for a free second mailing; accepting a personal gift in return for awarding a contract or making a major purchase; falsely noting neck or back pain after being in a rear end collision; and on and on.**

> **Are any of these close to something you are familiar with? No? Read on. Corruption in the business world is advertising to use a certain quality of oil when servicing a car, but substituting a cheaper grade; it is shaving a point or two off a final score of a basketball game to get over or under the point spread used in wagers; it is claiming to want to release a blocked payment if only the recipient could transfer enough money to pay the export license fee; and it is every other scam and fraud that one person foists on another.**

What harm is there, some might ask, in doing something like shaving a point or two off a final score? Just miss a free throw in the second half or send up a brick in the last few seconds. Your team still racks up a "W," but so does the gambler and so does the cooperating player with nice clothes and perhaps a car in return. Everybody wins? Right?

Wrong. This type of "harmless" corruption that can be so facilely justified is the same type of corruption that changes the moral fabric of a country. It is a spiral that becomes hard to slow let alone stop. As noted in a book I wrote in 2004 titles, *Corruption:*

> *. . . nothing seems to impede the flood of corrupt activities. All the new laws, added guards, higher fences, extra black boxes, increased audits, additional monitors, bigger signs and tougher . . . penalties have proven ineffective [in halting them.]*

The rewards of cheating plus the number of officials charged with ending corruption who themselves are cheating the system are nearly overwhelming. I concluded the Introduction to the second edition of *Corruption* with this thought:

> *We believe that until each of us is ready to exhibit some genuine anger at the corrupt activities that surround us, until each of us finds the will and a way to penalize those who perpetuate any type of corruption, until each of us is ready to end our own corrupt behaviors, we will never get a societal cure. In short, as Shakespeare might have noted, the fault, dear reader, is not in our stars, but in ourselves.*

The sad part is that a dozen years after writing

those words, they still hold true. The even sadder truth is that lobbycratic governance cannot be reversed until individuals take the same kind of pledge to fully participate in their government as every democracy requires.

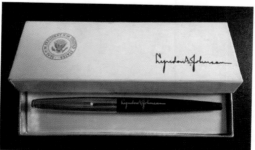

Godfrey Harris receiving one of the pens (a Tip-Wic Ever-sharp by the Parker Pen Company) used by President Lyndon Johnson in signing the Department of Transportation bill in the White House East Room on October 15, 1966.

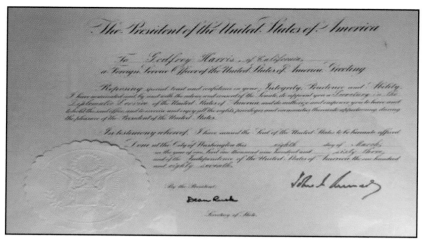

Godfrey Harris's commission as a United States Foreign Service Officer signed by President Kennedy and Secretary of State Dean Rusk in 1961 with the Great Seal of the United States attesting to the authenticity of the document affixed..

'Well, Once They Started With Parking Meters And Bus-Stop Shelters . . .'

The *St. Louis Post Dispatch* having gentle fun with a parking meter advertising concept advanced by the author as a new funding source for cities.

A certificate presented by the City of Los Angeles to Godfrey Harris for organizing an event honoring the role that collectors play in our culture.

Godfrey Harris served as Executive Consultant to the American Revolution Bicentennial Commission, the agency charged with planning the 200th anniversary of the Declaration of Independence. Here President Richard Nixon greets Harris at the White House in 1969 with Stanford University Chancellor Wally Sterling, in the background, making the introduction of a fellow Californian to the President.

Godfrey Harris took former California governor, Edmund G. "Pat" Brown, to the Nixon Library in Yorba Linda, Ca. Brown toured the facility before speaking by phone with President Nixon for the first time since they ran against each other for governor in 1962.

Ambassador James Roosevelt and Godfrey Harris meet on the tarmac of Geneva Airport in 1968 when both served as private diplomats for Investors Overseas Services, an international investment firm specializing in mutual funds.

The Los Angeles County Board of Supervisors presented the author, shown with his wife, Barbara DeKovner-Mayer, a certificate of appreciation for arranging to have a an oversized mural honoring the moon landing printed and displayed in a county facility.

7.

THE AMERICAN
LEGAL SYSTEM

Nearly every aspect of American governance is widely discussed today by the chattering classes in person, on talk radio, in newspaper columns and through postings on social media. About 15 percent of the population seems to care and comment consistently on such public policy matters as the status of health care, the quality of education, the changes in the economy, the strength of national security, America's standing in the world, the impact of illegal drugs, the reality of undocumented immigration, the pace of cultural change, the value of supporting the arts, and other such topics.

But these active participants in all things governmental have little to say about the state of America's *legal* system. That's because a lot of them are tied hand, foot and finger to its tentacles.

Oh, yes, most of the chattering class note major Supreme Court decisions. They are widely reported and their broad implications discussed for a day or two. But the topic soon fades from the top of the list of aspects of American life of most concern to its leadership. Yet no other subject probably has the potential of affecting so many people so consistently as the legal system.

Perhaps Philip K. Howard, writing in the *The Wall Street Journal,* expressed it best when he noted:

> *What's broken is American law — a man-made mountain of outdated statutes and regulations. Bad laws trap daily decisions in legal concrete and are largely responsible for the U.S. government's clunky ineptitude.*

Here are a few examples of what Howard has found that makes government so sloth-like:

- Fully 11,000 pages have been added to the Code of Federal Regulations during the presidency of Barack Obama — and the count has accelerated as he approaches the end of his term. Among the additions and changes are some very controversial actions taken by the President under his executive authority. Some of the changes are under challenge in the Supreme Court as beyond his constitutional authority.

* One of these is designed to help the U.S. immigration system become "more fair and more just." Under the President's Executive Orders, an estimated four million individuals in the United States illegally — including those who have children who are U.S. citizens — will have the opportunity to apply for work documents to remain in this country legally.

* The Obamacare mandate to provide contraceptives to those who request them was *not* part of the original Affordable Care Act as lawyers for the Catholic bishops point out. The provision was *added* by the Obama Administration in an Executive Order following Congressional passage of the law.

- Retired law professor John Baker wrote in *The Wall Street Journal* in 2011 that "there is no one in the United over the age of 18 who cannot be indicted for some federal crime!" Although there was no exclamation point in the original article, I have added one here to emphasize the ever-present potential role that the legal system plays in the lives of every person in the United States.

- Congressman Jim Sensenbrenner adds another ominous note about the legal system: "[Given the] . . . risk of violating obscure laws or rules, staying out of prison and avoiding fines and legal fees depends on the arbitrary whims of a bureaucrat."

* As an example, Sensenbrenner cites a family in Virginia who were assessed a $535 fine in 2011 when their young daughter saved an injured woodpecker. That was deemed by a Federal agency to be a "taking or transporting" of a protected species — illegal according to the Federal Migratory Bird Act. The agency later apologized for its heavy handed response, but the technocratic insensibility stands as a model of what the American people now face in lobbycratic governance.

* More startling is the story of Abner Schoenwetter who was found guilty in the year 2000 of packaging lobsters in plastic containers rather than cardboard — a violation of the laws of *Honduras*. Under the U.S. Lacey Act of 1900, it is illegal for an American citizen to violate any fish or wildlife regulation of *another* nation. Schoenwetter spent six years in a federal prison for what he did.

Yes, we all know that *ignorantia juris non excusat* — ignorance of the law is no excuse. But only a lawyer anxious to provide his legal advice to all comers could enforce such a dictum, especially when the law in question is Honduran(!) and is made applicable to US citizens by a statute that is more than 100 years old (!).

Since days of ancient Greece, philosophers, doctors, aristocrats, landowners and others served their societies in settling disputes. Today, of course, all that has changed. Lawyers now control everything to do with the American justice system:

- All judges are lawyers;

- All litigating attorneys are lawyers;

- A disproportionate share of legislators are lawyers — 64 percent of Senators and 37 percent of Representatives in the 114th Congress.

- All lawyers have attended law schools effectively controlled by other lawyers.

- All law schools teach the same subjects to their students using a similar syllabus.

- All students of the law are required to pass an examination, prescribed by lawyers, to test their knowledge of the law as those lawyers deem sufficient in order to practice law with and against them in each state.[†]

Can you name another American profession that

[†]Even control of law school admissions is centralized in something called the Law School Admission Council. The Law School Admission Test (LSAT) is under challenge by the University of Arizona Law School, which has decided to use the Graduate Record Examination (GRE) to qualify law school applicants. This heresy has been met by a threat to cut Arizona out of the applicant pipeline. The intensity of the battle suggests how much lawyers want to continue to control every aspect of the American legal system.

has gained such complete control over its environment, its work product, its income stream and its professional standards? None, as far as I have been able to discover — not architects, not engineers, not doctors, not contractors, not by other professional group.

As a result of this virtual monopoly over a vital part of our governance, all lawyers operate their practices in essentially the same way with the same goals, the same expectations, the same income sources and the same exaggerated view of their value to their fellow citizens.

Nationally, all members of the Senate Judiciary Committee, ever since the committee was first formed in the early 19th century, have been lawyers. All members of the Supreme Court and all federal judges are lawyers, even though a philosopher, a doctor, a scientist or a theologian might provide a more balanced view of the underlying meaning of a constitutional phrase or the laws touching it.

All professional litigators, in order to be able to appear in federal, state and local courts, have to be addmitted by a local bar association. No, everyone points out, a defendant can represent himself in a criminal trial. True, and it wasn't for nothing that a lawyer devised the self-serving statement that he who has himself for a client has a fool for a lawyer. The system is rigged for bar associations.

Talk about a closed system with its own rules and arcane ways. Individuals who have had an issue playing out in the U.S. court system know that it was not designed for administrative efficiency or to expedite the resolution of the matter for the litigants; it is a system designed for the professional convenience of all the lawyers involved. Things start and stop according to *their* schedules. Ask anyone who has been a witness in a legal proceeding or hung around for hours waiting to be considered for jury duty.

A majority of federal and state legislators devising our laws, approving judicial appointments and setting judicial salaries are lawyers. Is it any wonder, then, that we have singled out lawyers for special attention in a discussion of the real ways that U.S. government is now run and controlled?

THE TRUTH OF LEGAL HUMOR

Anytime a fresh lawyer joke begins skipping through incoming email boxes, knowing smiles, nodding heads and forwarded messages blossom. It is acknowledgement of the humor's underlying truth. For example, this one arrived not long ago:

A lawyer dies in a car accident on his 40th birthday and finds himself at the Pearly Gates. A brass band is playing, the angels are singing, and everyone wants to shake his hand. Just when he thinks things can't possibly get any better, Saint Peter himself comes over, apologizes for not greeting him personally on his arrival, and says, "We've been waiting a long time for you.

"We're celebrating the fact that you lived to be 160 years old! God himself wants to meet with you!" The lawyer is awestruck and says "Saint Peter, I lived my life in the eternal hope that when I died I would

163

be judged by God and be found to be worthy, but I only lived to be forty years old."

"That's simply impossible," says Saint Peter. "We've added up all of your client time sheets."

Here is another one along the same lines of lawyers and money, but a little less subtle.

An old miser, due to his terrible cheapness, had neither friends nor family. Just before he died he called his doctor, his lawyer and a minister to visit him. They complied, and gathered together around his bed.

"I always heard you can't take it with you, but I am going to prove you can," he said. "I have $90,000 cash hidden underneath my mattress. It's in three envelopes of $30,000 each. I want each one of you to take one envelope now and just before they throw the dirt on my coffin, you throw the envelopes in."

Weeks later, the three attended the miser's funeral, and true to their word, each threw an envelope into the grave. On the way back from the cemetery, the minister said, "I don't feel so good about this. I desperately needed $10,000 to fix the plumbing in our church to make it handicap accessible, so I took out $10,000 and threw only $20,000 in the grave."

The doctor said, "I, too, must confess. I am building a new extension for our clinic and took $20,000. I threw in the balance of $10,000." He looked ashamed.

The lawyer said, "Gentlemen, I'm surprised, shocked and disappointed in both of you. I don't see how you could in good conscience hold on to that money. I threw in a personal check for the entire amount."

Did a smile come across your face? The one about the time sheets reminded me of a situation a few years back when we engaged a lawyer to collect a debt for us in his area. The lawyer told us his hourly rate was $430. Okay, we thought, he comes highly recommended as someone who could solve our problem quickly.

I soon learned that he broke every billing hour into tenths, the law firm's minimum charge. Fair enough, I thought when I signed the engagement letter. But that attitude changed after the first invoice arrived. A spate of those tenths of an hour, it turned out, were devoted to receiving or sending emails about our case.

At a cost of $43 just to *open* an email (don't you wish you got that kind of money for that daily chore?), we wanted every communication to count. But when I learned that the lawyer copied everyone involved in the case on every email he received and sent — claiming an ethical duty to keep all parties fully informed — I went slightly crazy. It was not that I objected to the broad distribution of information on details of our unfolding case, but some of the recipients were incapable of allowing any email to arrive without making some acknowledgment of having read and understood it. These are the ones that send those automatic, meaningless responses and innocuous comments of "Thank you," "OK," "Got it" or "Done" to every cc who received the original. Have any of these types in your email chain?

They proved costly to us. I couldn't blame the lawyer for opening every one of these emails to see if there was anything of substantive value, but it was costing us a fortune at $43 a pop since the lawyer seemed to review the emails when he had a break from his other cases.

It was a funding fountain for the lawyer and his firm that proved impossible to turn off, slow down or eliminate. I soon was looking for another lawyer with the stipulation that I would not be charged for *reading* any incoming email, only for the time it took to craft a substantive reply of direct relevance to our case. I found one who agreed to the condition and engaged her. She and her colleagues eventually won a settlement in the matter and got us some of the money we were owed.

It is an experience like ours that can spark so much legal humor, except, perhaps, among those with lawyers in their families. When was the last time you read, heard or participated in a substantive review of the positive influence of lawyers on the American system of governance? In the famous words of the Gilbert and Sullivan song in *H.M.S. Pinafore* discussing the qualifications of the First Lord of the Admiralty, "Hardly ever."

There is a reason the American legal system pro-vides so much fodder for humor — the points ring true with so many people. Consider these three:

- *A small town that cannot support one lawyer can always support two.*

- *Lawyers write a 10,000-word document and call it a brief, then chafe at page limitations.*

- *The judicial process is like a cow. The public is impaled on its horns, the government has it by the tail, and the lawyers are milking it.*

THE LAWYERING SYSTEM

Long ago barbers transformed themselves into surgeons and printers became publishers — all in the interest of realizing a greater profit from essentially the same basic services they had always provided to their customers. The only difference with lawyers today is that they built a legal protected monopoly in the process of establishing their importance to society.

As a result, most seem more concerned about making money than finding justice. Lawyers charge too much because they control a closed system that deters real competition in conflict resolution, property protection or the maintenance of individual rights. In fact, working the legal system for profit can be so lucrative that litigation has become a hot investment vehicle. *The Wall Street Journal* reported in May 2016 that "pension funds, university endowments, family [foundations] have . . . pumped more than a billion dollars into the sector . . ."

Here is another example of how the closed legal system works:

> A giant Chicago law firm habitually mailed our Los Angeles-based company a one-page report on the progress of a bankruptcy proceeding accompanied by a 30-page(!) single sided listing of everyone receiving the report. The law firm, it seemed, had created a captive company to provide mailing services

for the cost of that work plus a fixed profit percentage awarded by the court. The bigger the package and the heavier the mailing, the higher the costs involved, and therefore the greater the profit to the law firm's partners.

Stuffing, addressing and stamping a large flat envelope with dozens of pages of material costs more than posting a small business envelope with one or two sheets of machine-folded paper. Six percent applied against the higher cost associated with the bigger envelope produces a lot more money than the same percentage applied against one first class letter.

We protested vigorously that the list of those served could be put in three columns and the list printed back-to-back on both sides of the paper. The bankruptcy judge dismissed our suggestion as if it were beneath his dignity to deal with, passed our suggestion to the lawyers (who ignored it), and then routinely approved the law firm's invoices filled with bloat and waste — the usual lawyer-to-lawyer courtesy at the expense of everyone else involved with the system.

LAWYERS IN GOVERNANCE

The closed legal system has also allowed lawyers to occupy a crucial role in the operation of lobbycratic governance. Note these points.

- Every major organization within American society — government agencies, publicly traded companies, large interest groups —

either have a coterie of lawyers on staff or independent firms on call to provide counsel on what is permitted under the law, what may not be and what could be done to do what the executive wants to do within existing law or if need be under a proposed new law.

- Attend any board of education meeting, any planning commission session, any law making or rule making body — even a hearing on a traffic ticket — and note how pervasive is the official role that lawyers play in the decisions being made.

- Every document issued by a governmental organization, every activity that touches the public and every decision that has consequences for someone somewhere shows the fingerprints of a lawyer on the written statement and on the decision itself.

- Every agency of government either has counsel on hand for its public and private deliberations, finds its decisions subject to review by some legal authority somewhere, or can have any of its activities challenged in a court for their legality by other lawyers.

What's the problem, most would ask? Aren't the lawyers merely keeping the system operating properly between the lines that society originally drew for its activities? Aren't lawyers just making sure that government agencies are fulfilling the dictates found in the preamble to the United States Constitution:

". . . to form a more perfect Union, establish Justice, insure domestic Tranquility, provide for the common defence, promote the general Welfare, and secure the Blessings of Liberty to ourselves and our Posterity"?

Aren't lawyers just soldiers in the constant battle to ensure that American government operates under the established rules? Don't they have to be vigilant against the whims of individuals in charge to do whatever they please? Aren't all of these worthy undertakings?

They are. But lawyers are not cousins of the Wizard of Oz, blessed with mystical powers of wisdom and judgment. They are men and women subject to all the prejudices, biases and foibles of everyone else. They can be as easily corrupted as any other person — and some would say more so because they understand how to bend the rules without necessarily breaking them. It is the reason we have to be vigilant of their power over the system they have have helped create.

LAWYERING AS BUSINESS

Lawyers, of course, are also subject to the same economic forces as everyone else — looking for work and fees to take care of family and office. Because they are directly involved in how society operates, we acquiesce when they use the system they helped develop to do what they have been trained to do — use the system to the advantage of their clients.

And that is the reason for the pervasiveness of lawyers in our lives. We have come to the point that absolutely everything is now legally questionable by some member of the bar under some rule, regulation or interpretation. Show me a lawyer who isn't eager to take another battle into a courtroom or boardroom — as long as a path to paying his or her fees is visible and viable. And note this: The battle the lawyers are fighting is not necessarily one for justice, as many lawyers would have us believe, but is just as often a battle primarily against those with deep enough pockets to pay the fees that lawyers now command or to settle the matter for sums that make the effort worthwhile.

Litigation in the United States has become so pervasive and so expensive that modern day bouncers and doormen no longer use force to remove the unruly from clubs, bars and queues. They are now taking courses on how to maintain order without inviting lawsuits from those thrown out of a venue or line for unseemly behavior. The course is not inexpensive, but then again neither are the lawsuits for assault and other infractions that can result in a heavy handed end to a confrontation.

A few years after I had blanched at those $430 per hour fees, an organization I was managing was asked to contribute to another legal pool to fund another lawyer opposing the wording of a government regulation. I was informed that this Washington lawyer's fees are $1,030 an hour! By 2016, according to the *Wall Street Journal*, the fee for the very highest paid lawyers in America had breached the $1,500 per hour mark. For those of you not willing to do the math, that is a sum that would help a fully engaged lawyer approach an income level of $30 million per year.

The high cost of legal advice, of course, is not new. Thomas Fleming describes what America was really like in 1776. Among the statistics is this note that "it took about 500 pounds a year — about $40,000 [in today's dollars] — for a family to feel well off. Skilled workers, such as carpenters, earned around 90 pounds [$5,000] annually. Schoolteachers made little more than a landless laborer." Fleming then adds: "At the top of the economic pyramid were lawyers." They made as much as 3,000 pounds a year — equal to $240,000 in today's dollars.

Business people have long railed against the activities of trial lawyers seeking to form groups of people to make claims against wealthy defendants in class action suits. These are the lawyers who are not interested in a court case so much as a settlement and who use the media to embarrass a defendant to make it cheaper to close out a case than to contest the claims before a jury.

Attorneys general, district attorneys and other lawyers for the government do the same thing: Charge some prominent citizen or major corporation with a list of crimes only to settle the matter later and quietly by agreeing that the crimes were not so bad after all and a lesser level of punishment would satisfy the needs of "justice." In these cases, of course, the government lawyers get to puff their win/loss statistics on the way to a judgeship, partnership or book deal; the citizen walks away saving a lot of time, money and the possibility that the state might have convinced a judge or jury that whatever happened was sufficiently injurious to society to warrant a huge fine or prison time.

UNSETTLING SETTLEMENTS

Lawyers don't want to win cases in court replicating Charles Darrow or the mythical Perry Mason; they seem to want to settle matters to enhance their fame and glory and to provide reasonable satisfaction to their clients who will then pay for their efforts. Look at this partial list of recent settlements:

- In 2016, Goldman Sachs agreed to pay a $5 billion settlement over allegations it knowingly sold faulty mortgage securities to investors. Goldman Sachs manages nearly $1 trillion in assets, and the settlement was structured in a way that allows the company to write off $2.6 billion — more than half — as a tax deduction.[†] In addition, most of the consumer relief actions in the settlement (valued at $1.8 billion) are not

---

[†]Tax deductibility, of course, is another way of saying tax savings. Goldman Sacks will save about $875 million of the fine by *not* paying taxes on its other income. The bottom line is that the punishment is not as harsh or as expensive as the headline number would suggest. Why? Brandon Garrett, professor at the University of Virginia School of Law, has said that the Department of Justice has never given a good explanation for why it has allowed tax-deductible settlements in these cases. One tax lawyer speculates that the DOJ receives up to 3 percent of a *total* settlement for its Working Capital Fund, a slush fund for agency activities and shared administrative services. The bigger the total settlement, before deductions, the larger the likely share for the technocrats and bureaucrats to use. How's that for a corrupt little secret? Do you need any more proof why lobbycratic governance remains so strong?

truly cash expenditures, but the restructuring of home loans to help consumers avoid future foreclosures.

Alan Pyke of ThinkProgress analyzed the Goldman Sacks deal in this way: "[It]is the latest in a long line of settlements where... admitting guilt [is avoided] ... and ... the actual cost of securing . . . freedom from both corporate and individual prosecution [is minimized]. Previous government deals [have been] with JP Morgan, Bank of America, Citibank, Morgan Stanley, and others."

- In 2016, British Petroleum agreed to pay more than $20 billion to settle claims over the 2010 oil spill in the Gulf of Mexico. It is estimated BP will be able to deduct over $15 billion (three-fourths) from the settlement because these costs were expressly classified as ordinary business expenses for environmental recovery — not a fine.

- GlaxoSmithKline, one of the big pharmaceutical companies, negotiated a $3 billion settlement with the Department of Justice in 2012 for health care fraud related to promoting its antidepressants for unapproved uses, improper marketing and failing to report safety data. No individuals were prosecuted or forced to resign, and $3 billion represents only 10 percent of what GlaxoSmithKline is believed to have earned on the sale of the drugs. According to advocacy group "Taxpayers Against Fraud," "a $3 billion settlement for half a dozen drugs over 10 years can be rationalized as . . . [just another] cost of doing business."

In other cases, government lawyers are settling for large amounts to protect the reputation of past or present technocrats or save the government from certain embarrassment. Here is a look at a few of these cases.

- The US Government paid the Navajo Nation $554 million in 2014 to settle a mismanagement claim. The Indian tribe said that the government had failed to negotiate appropriate extraction deals for natural resources, had not ensured that the Navajo Nation would get full royalties, and had not invested the proceeds for maximum profits. Nice. The Interior Department used taxpayer money to ensure that any corruption, leadership failure or malfeasance would never surface in a courtroom. And as Dennis Kelleher, head of a financial watchdog group called Better Markets, has said: ". . . there's an endless reservoir of ways . . . to hold no one accountable for illegal conduct."

- In 2016, the U.S. government agreed to pay $1.7 billion to Iran to settle a decades-long legal claim. Prior to the Iranian Revolution, Iran had set up a $400 million trust fund for the purchase of military equipment. This money was frozen when diplomatic relations were severed between the two countries in 1979. But with the 2015 agreement to limit Iran's development of its nuclear capability, the U.S. agreed to return the money with interest. A high ranking U.S.

official told reporters that the settlement is "in the U.S. interest . . . to reduce our risk of liability." For what? No one explained, the press ignored the comment, and the public shrugged.[†]

- Just a *day*(!) after Boeing filed a lawsuit, the federal government agreed to pay the company $32.25 million to avoid litigation over whether the government or Boeing was really responsible for polluting a site in Wichita, Kansas. The money covers past and future costs of cleaning up soil and groundwater from when the government owned the site and was involved in manufacturing activities. Sounds like another legal settlement to stop embarrassing details from being revealed about who might have been responsible for either the sloppy or the purposeful handling of hazardous materials. Technocrats taking care of themselves and their bureaucratic colleagues.

- In 2012 the U.S. government agreed to pay $350,000 to 11 men for an immigration raid in New Haven, Connecticut. According to Fox News Latino, the men were forced at gunpoint out of their beds and their homes. The men claimed Immigration and Customs Enforcement was retaliating against New Haven for its

---

[†] In standard American usage, whenever politicians refuse to be associated with an embarrassing or controversial decision, a "senior government official" is the chosen source for a news story. That was always Henry Kissinger's favorite cover. Could Secretary of State John Kerry have adopted it here for his own purposes? Sounds plausible..

176

status as a "sanctuary city" for undocumented immigrants. They said they were targeted solely because of their Latino appearance. ICE had indeed screwed up but as usual no single official was ever identified as responsible for the error.

- As a worthy example of numerous cases in which prosecutorial excess or legal misconduct resulted in someone spending jail time for a wrongful conviction, New York City settled a lawsuit for $40 million for five people who were in prison for murder and spent more than 17 years behind bars.

LAWYERING IN THE UNITED STATES

The point is that the legal system in the United States now gives the appearance of working more for the benefit of lthe government than the protection of the citizenry. The lawyers deny it and claim that all those who oppose their profession don't understand it, have been hurt by it, have failed at it or really wish they could have been part of it.

Perhaps some of that is true, but look at the facts about lawyering in the United States today.

Lobbycratic governance needs the cooperation of lawyers at nearly every step of every process to give the work that lobbyists and technocrats do the control they want and the sheen of legitimacy they grave.

Like much else that has happened in America, the ascendancy of lawyers occurred slowly and organically: A power was asserted and when no one took strong enough umbrage or generated enough opposition to it, the power became accepted and then embedded in the system for maintaining peace and good order for society.

Some lawyers, of course, have recognized the problem and have been in the forefront of trying to reform the justice system. We now have small claims courts, fast-track procedures, private judges, arbitration hearings, mandatory settlement conferences, and the like. But since so many of these procedures require both sides to agree in their use and demand substantial resources to pay for these special judicial procedures, they cannot solve all the disputes that arise in a society. In addition, the new procedures don't deal with the multiple evils of long delays, large claims, high costs and collection problems that continue to bedevil the system.

SOLVING THE LAWYERING PROBLEM

We need to democratize the law profession by allowing non-lawyers to sit on the highest courts. We need to broaden legal education to include more non-legal subjects — philosophy, psychology, biology, art history, music theory, and more. Laymen ought to be involved in all decision making concerning the profession — in law school entry requirements, curricula, disciplinary activities, testing and the like.

Most of all, we need to end the monopoly that lawyers have assumed in interpreting the law. Non-lawyers write many of the laws; non-lawyers sign the laws as President, governors and mayors.

Why do lawyers, then, have to be the only ones to interpret the meaning of a law?

Lawyers have maintained their monopoly over all things legal for too many years. Take the role of notaries public, those anachronistic remnants of the 19th century whose basic job these days is to authenticate the identity of signatories to documents and administer oaths. In nearly all cases, notaries accept a driver's license as proof that a person is who he or she says they are. But how easy is it for anyone to obtain a driver's license today using a stolen or even made up identity?

In California, notaries who are lawyers are allowed to give a full range of advice to individuals on the documents they are processing. Non-lawyer notaries are strictly prohibited from giving any such advice. Who decided this? If you guessed that lawyers in the Secretary of State's office created the distinction, wrote the regulations and determined what notaries can and cannot do, you guessed right.

To that point, I have been a notary public in California for the past 15 years. As such, I am well aware that I am not allowed to make any comments on any aspect of a document that I am notarizing. Lawyers of course can. Yet as a public policy consultant, I give advice all the time to clients on legislation, regulations and every other aspect of government policy without any oversight.

I was once refused a renewal of my notarial credentials because I had left off my date of birth on a required form. Tough, said the California Secretary of State's office. I had failed to complete a required form in its entirety. Wrong, I argued. They knew my date of birth by virtue of my original application and subsequent renewals. This was an inadvertent error, a technical mistake, not a substantive one worthy of disqualifying someone. I won the battle through persistence, but not until I had involved a member of the Assembly with budget power over the Secretary of State's office to intervene on my behalf.

There are dozens of stories of how lawyers take care of their own. That might even be praiseworthy except for the fact that they have extraordinary power to do more than take care of other lawyers. Take judges who are asked to award attorney fees in various class action, bankruptcy and other proceedings. Since all judges once were practicing lawyers somewhere in the system, they are understanding and generous with their brethren seeking funds to meet payrolls and office expenses. They have been there, suffered that and struggled as well. The individual or entity having to pay the cost of the fees awarded are no match for the sympathetic hearing a fellow lawyer gets in front of the bench.

This ought to end. Financial awards to lawyers should be made on objective grounds by non-lawyers. This would be a first step in ending the monopoly that lawyers have assumed for every aspect of their profession.

> Finally, we need to end the insistence that only lawyers are allowed to practice law. Paralegals, like physicians assistants, can be

wills, review contracts, represent clients in negotiations and make court appearances to answer judicial inquiries. They, like notaries, ought to be legally empowered to give advice to those who ask. If a lawyer protests that a non-lawyer might give a client wrong advice, ask how many courts have overturned criminal sentences because of incompetent legal representation and ask how many lawyers have been sued for malpractice because of giving wrong advice. In short, having a law license does not necessarily guarantee sound counsel.

While some lawyers would have us believe that only they should be allowed to give advice because of their superior training, the fact is that they are simply protecting their turf from intrusion from anyone who has not passed the bar examination. Lawyers have always hated the thought of competition among their brethren, thinking it undignified and not in keeping with their august calling.

However, when they learned how much more money could be made from an expanded client pool developed through advertising — permitted after a Supreme Court case — they adjusted that particular prejudice to accommodate to the new order. So the public, in our view, ought to demand that more non-lawyers get involved in the legal business as a way to bring down the protected, monopolistic and in many cases unequal contingency fees in order to serve the average person.

LICENSING OTHER PROFESSIONS

Although we have concentrated on the control the legal profession has been able to exert over governance within the United States, let us not forget that it is only symptomatic of another aspect of government activity: Licensing by state authorities of professional activities and consumer services. This has had a profound influence on how these activities are conducted, the price paid for services rendered and what kinds of innovations can be made.

If lawyers control the bar associations which set the standards for legal practice within a state, what about the other agencies that set standards of competence for other pursuits — such as doctors, contractors, beauty salons, locksmiths, electricians and everything else? How much is the public involved in the decisions that these licensing agencies make and how much is dependent on what the lobbyists representing professional groups can do in conjunction with the technocrats who work for the relevant oversight agencies?

Along these lines, please take note of another whole level of government in the United States that the media ignores for the most part, the politicians steer clear of and the public pays little mind to. They are the regional governments and special districts that deal with libraries, roads, fire prevention, lighting, parks, schools and on and on. They are formed primarily as a taxing entity and then use the funds collected or borrowed to build and maintain facilities for public use. They are a happy hunting grounds for lawyers who specialize in the minutiae that these agencies deal with. Take Florida.

Florida has nearly 1,000(!) special districts that

raise and spend over $7 billion in public funds annually. There are 136 districts, many run by unelected boards, that can impose property taxes on homeowners and businesses in one or more counties. There are no requirements for those who deal regularly with these districts to disclose their activities. Audubon Florida's director gave an example of how free-wheeling these districts can be:

> *There are consultants to the sugar industry who are spending time with and influencing the thinking of [the] South Florida Water Management District governing board members. . . . they [aren't] registered as lobbyists. . .We see them, but it's too shadowy to know exactly what they're doing.*

As if to highlight how sloppy government can become without some level of oversight responsible ultimately to the people, the same South Florida Water Management District spent $1.5 million on 15 electric pumps in 2007. The pumps failed; the manufacturer refused to honor the warranty. Later, it was revealed that the lawyer for the pump company also worked as its chief lobbyist. Not unusual, but what was stunning was the fact that he was also vice chairman of the district's nine-member governing board. How's that for self dealing?

Lobbyists are particularly drawn to Florida's special districts because they have governing power over public works projects associated with planned communities. That means that everything from infrastructure decisions to lawn mowing services are determined by a board that can be influenced to see the world in the same way as a lobbyist sees the same world for his clients.

So much, in fact, of what governments do to impact the lives of its citizenry has almost nothing to do with Congress or the President. Lobbycratic governance is alive and well not only in Washington but in small towns all across the country. It is just another example of why today's government is no where close to your father's government.

8.
SOME MORE ILLUSTRATIVE ISSUES

This chapter is about some of the issues currently confronting the American people and how lobby-cratic governance changes the way we deal with them. In the days of Lyndon Johnson, the issues he wanted to solve were large and complex, but there was a pattern to how the government addressed its policy needs. It was, in fact, the government of your fathers.

In those days, the President articulated the policy goals for his administration, had his staff communicate those ideas to his cabinet and the independent agencies of the federal government, and then worked on the political details with key members of the House and Senate. A few bills began on the Hill and were adopted by the administration; most, however, were drafted by the executive branch agencies with subsequent input from the White House.

Eventually a finished bill was formally introduced by a friendly senator or representative. Once the bill was made part of the Congressional machinery, lobbyists and other interested citizens had ample time to informally discuss their concerns with individual senators or representatives or testify for or against the bill in a committee session. Throughout, the White House was kept informed and together with the Congressional leadership made the changes and adjustments in wording that resulted in a final piece of legislation moving toward Presidential signature with maximum agreement.

DEPARTMENT OF TRANSPORTATION

Take the Department of Transportation. When Lyndon Johnson came to the Presidency, the U. S. was the only major country in the world lacking a centralized authority to oversee and coordinate the development and safety of all modes of transportation. Johnson thought that was not only shortsighted, but wrong for the economy.

He also decided the federal purview over transportation should not be limited to rail, road and air. Lyndon Johnson saw the opportunity to coordinate pipeline networks, bus lines and rivers, canals and coastal waterways. Elevators were not part of the transportation network he envisaged — even though they carry more Americans per day than any other mode of transportation. I now think that had the subject arisen in 1966, he would have been intrigued by the surprise element it would have offered to keep his opponents guessing on what else could be included in the bill.

While Eisenhower is famously remembered for wanting to duplicate the German autobahn system across the U.S. with a network of interconnecting federal highways, jurisdiction for these roadways was in the hands of the Secretary of Commerce. John F. Kennedy never saw any advantage in consolidating transportation units into one agency; after all, he had selected former Pan-American Airlines CEO and father of Queen Noor of Jordan, Najeeb Halaby, to run the powerful Federal Aviation Agency. Najeeb gave the administration some glamour as well as connectivity to the Middle East. No sense in burying that within a large bureaucracy.

But once President Johnson saw the chance to consolidate the transportation agencies to better coordinate all outdoor modes of transportation for the benefit of the economy, he was all over it. He believed the country would be better off when the Maritime Administration competed directly for budget dollars with the FAA; he liked the idea of taking the Coast Guard from Treasury to emphasize its safety mission over its revenue collection duties.

But there was huge bureaucratic blowback to the idea. The Coast Guard provided the Secretary of Treasury with air transportation for short haul flights as well as mess facilities in the Treasury

Building; the FAA liked its independence and liked its new building better — a building fatefully opened on November 23, 1963. The agency technocrats didn't want to give up the coveted big view top floor offices to the staff of the new Secretary of Transportation. They wanted it for themselves.

Paul Hall, head of the Seafarers International Union, was also opposed to Lyndon's new department. He knew how to work the Department of Commerce to get attention and budget dollars for programs that helped his members. How would he relate to the new department? How many other unions would be competing for Secretarial attention? He decided he wanted to stay in Commerce and to fight the move to the new department. When Johnson heard that Hall was staying put, he exploded with some of his most famous invective — including a roaring reference to cutting off his balls for daring to oppose his President. But Paul Hall avoided castration because on this issue he had more juice — money and local votes — with members of the Congress. Maritime stayed put. And Lyndon took his political lumps philosophically. Okay, he told us, we got most of what we wanted; we'll get the rest in a little while.

The creation of a Department of Transportation was first proposed in Lyndon Johnson's State of the Union Address of 1966. A few days later, the Budget Bureau, working with Joseph Califano, the President's principal legislative aide, sent a bill to Congress. Nine months later the legislation was approved. A picture of the author, then a member of the Office of Management in the Budget Bureau, being thanked by the President at the bill's signing ceremony can be seen at page 153.

In the 2015 reprinting of his book *The Triumph and Tragedy of Lyndon Johnson: The White House Years,* Joe Califano shows how much government of the day was done by legislation. As Califano notes:

> *Lyndon Johnson certainly meant to tilt the balance of power to the White House, not only vis-à-vis the other branches of the federal government, but also vis-à-vis the states, cities and counties. He saw this shift as essential in order to deal with the hard rock of resistance to his civil rights and anti-poverty measures. And, of course, it fit nicely into his personal penchant for power. In fact, his great society programs have also enhanced the power of Congress, something he would have regarded as collateral damage.*
>
> *Thus, a lasting legacy [of the Johnson Administration] is that not just the Presidency but the Congress for good or ill became a locus of power, displacing the states, cities and institutions whose relative power has declined. As a result, the failures of the President and the Congress loom larger [now] because the power and our expectations have become larger.*

Now a half-century beyond the Johnson years, the ascendancy of lobbycratic governance has replaced the evermore dominant Presidency he created.

THE DIFFERENT WORLD OF WASHINGTON
Whatever one's view of big government in Washington, most Americans, the media and the political

elite accept it as reality. Today, the nation's capital is the go-to place where one after another of the lobbyists for major organizations seek governmental intervention for one commercial, social or political purpose or another.

It is clear how much has changed since Lyndon Johnson's era. Note these statistics:

- In his five years in office, Johnson got approval for more than 96 major bills that changed the face of America — Medicare, Civil Rights, Voting Rights, Arts and Humanities Foundation, War on Poverty, and more. Of course, as Rabbi Jerry Cutler of the Creative Arts Temple in Los Angeles put it in mid-2016: ". . . if we kept the 10 Commandments we would not need any more laws or prisons or punishments." Internet wags have floated their own reason why the 10 Commandments are known but not enforced: "We can't have rules such as 'Thou Shalt Not Steal,' 'Thou Shalt Not Commit Adultery' and 'Thou Shall Not Lie' in places full of judges and politicians — it creates a hostile work environment!"

- By the time of Bill Clinton, each President was looking at passing just *one* major piece of legislation during his term — reform of social welfare for Mr. Clinton, No Child Left Behind in Mr. Bush's tenure, and the Affordable Care Act during the Obama administration.

- The 115th Congress that begins in 2017 may be even less functional than recent legislative bodies. The Competitive Enterprise

Institute reports that over the past 40 years, Congress has produced an average of 282 bills a year for Presidential signature; the current Congress has managed only 114. But during this time — as if to prove the power of lobbycratic governance — more than 3,400 new *regulations* were issued requiring a staggering 80,260 pages in the *Federal Register*. Put simply, the lawyers figured out that detailed legislation of years gone by is no longer needed.

*   Why go through the agony and take the risk of losing on key elements when regulations issued to implement an existing law can be promulgated by an Executive branch agency and have the force of law once a new interpretation, definition, schedule, or other change is published in the *Federal Register*?

*   Big legislation is controversial and draws enormous energy from lobbying groups across the country. It isn't surprising that a comprehensive new tax code has not been created. Who has the stomach for the intense fight over thousands of details with real money at stake in every decision, every exception, every decimal point for decades to come?

*   If substantive legislation seems daunting and an Executive Order likely to draw too much comment, there is always the next *Budget Act* to direct or prohibit spending

that reflects whatever policy objective is sought. Using budgets to achieve substantive ends is not new, even if a dubious technique. Franklin Roosevelt created the Federal Writers' Project by funding it in the Emergency Relief Appropriation Act of 1935. Spending bills are now consolidated into year-end, rush-to-adjourn-before-Christmas, thousand-page behemoths that no one other than the technocrats and lobbyists read or understand.

It is a daunting exercise to determine the meaning of any element. Take this example from the 2015 Federal Budget Act:

(a) Revised Discretionary Spending Limits. Section 251(c) of the Balanced Budget and Emergency Deficit Control Act of 1985 (2 U.S.C. 901(c)) is amended by striking paragraphs (3) and (4) and inserting the following:``(3) for fiscal year 2016--``(A) for the revised security category, $548,091,000,000 in new budget authority; and ``(B) for the revised nonsecurity category $518,491,000,000 in new budget authority.

That sentence authorizes the expenditure of more than $1 trillion. Is that good or bad for the nation? Neither the people nor the politicians have a clue.

CURRENT NATIONAL ISSUES

The issues bothering the American people seem far removed from how the national media reports what the BIGS are worried about. It sets up the familiar refrain that politicians are tone deaf.

Presidential candidates in election campaigns are particularly prone to announcing non-solutions to the enthusiastic cheers of reliable supporters placed up front in the audience and behind the lectern to get maximum exposure to the television cameras. {"When I am President, I will fight for you on _____. [FILL IN THE BLANK WITH AN ISSUE BELOW]

- Health care
- Discrimination
- Immigration
- Education
- Environment
- Climate change
- College tuition
- Trade
- Debt relief

A popular alternative to "fighting" for some issue is the following sample pronouncement of a Presidential candidate: "Prohibiting unpaid internships will be my top priority on Day One in the Oval Office." Wild cheering from whatever group predominates in an audience. But did you catch any hints of an actual *solution* in the rhetoric? There were none, not even a realistic review of the politics of an issue.

Despite this, here is a list of what seems to be bothering *real* people (not political handlers listening to a focus group discussion) in the near term:

- While ISIS may not represent "an existential threat to the United States" it does make ordinary Americans fearful that their operatives or supporters could orchestrate another random attack anywhere at anytime — see 9/11, Madrid, Paris, Beirut, San Bernardino, Brussels, Ouagadougou, Orlando, and elsewhere.

- Some feel we must cut the federal deficit and the size of government at all levels before it consumes us. One individual called it "an enormous tumor eating away at the private sector and impacting the health and vigor of the economy."

- The Zika virus — a mosquito-borne disease that causes frightening disabilities in newborns — is spreading fast. In 2016, the Center for Disease Control and Prevention asked for $4.1 billion for vaccine development, education and mosquito abatement programs. The Republicans in Congress approved about 25 per cent of the request, arguing that other public health monies should be reprogrammed first — totally unconcerned that the average American is more worried by this disease than by future Iranian nuclear weapons or flooding of the Maldive Islands.

*   Some seek new legislation or regulations to:

  +   Allow Medicare to negotiate with pharmaceutical firms to lower drug costs.

  +   Dock the pay of legislators if federal

spending bills are not in place by the start of the fiscal year on October 1.

+ Increase the funding for more early education programs and child care.

* Yet another example of the mysteries of government today was the sudden *reduction* in postal rates in May 2016. After years of the Postal Service running huge deficits in an era of emails, social media communications and online bill paying, a rate reduction suddenly occurred without any change in the Service's financial fortunes. Was the two-cent reduction in first class rates merely *technical* in nature — the expiration of a temporary rate increase? Or was it really *political* in nature — an excuse to increase the financial distress of the Postal Service to drive it into the private sector to escape the financial burdens of its union contracts and the requirement to fully fund pension obligations ?

While some observers have admired the shrewdness of the move — when has the public ever complained about a price *reduction* for anything? — it points up how far removed the public has become from anything to do with government policy. The media is now too weak to report what was really behind the price reduction and the public too into its own concerns to press the issue. *The Wall Street Journal,* in an unrelated but revealing full page ad, noted that the made the changes and adjustments in wording that resulted in a final and to average person spends 71,400 minutes a year working after hours, but only five minutes a day reading what's news!

LOCAL ISSUES

Take education as an example of an important local government function that virtually embodies lobbycratic governance. Lobbyists for teachers and administrative staff, technocrats in the education industry from academia to publishing, and lawyers for all reflect the near triumph of non-elected and non-appointed specialists running a government program. Yet education is an area of public policy way too important to be left to educators alone.[†]

But BIGNESS in education works in a big way. The BIG educational unions, representing the certified teachers and supporting staff, contribute BIG

[†]Apropos this point, I have served in a number of voluntary capacities involved with education from a stint as chairman of the Santa Monica School Board's Mentally Gifted Minor Advisory Group to membership on the Coalition of (Los Angeles) High School Alumni Associations. This work brought me into contact with numerous professional educators. During those encounters, I looked for the chance to suggest that middle schoolers ought to be given a course in journalistic techniques as part of their English language requirements. I argued that everyone benefits from ensuring that each memo, letter, and Internet communication meets the time honored requirement of covering the WHO, WHAT, WHY, WHERE and WHEN of a topic. I can report that no one has ever given this idea more than a cursory nod, suggesting that since journalism is traditionally a high school subject and no professional educator has advocated the idea, adding it to a middle school curriculum would be an arduous undertaking. Nevertheless, I remain convinced that it ought to be discussed and considered.

money from collected dues to the campaigns for boards of education and for other offices. They, of course, support only those candidates known to favor union priorities — to a large extent, more independence from political interference, higher pay, more free time and smaller classes, increased classroom assistance in the form of aides, electronic equipment, and improved facility maintenance. Progress on any of these issues get union officers re-elected by their membership and enhanced their power in larger political arenas.

Once elected, more often than not with union support, members of a school board and / or the mayor of a city tend to appoint individuals to the educational bureaucracy that the unions favor. Should the union bosses become disenchanted with the performance of any of the elected officials they have supported, they can easily find someone else more pliant for the next election cycle. There are no shortage of ambitious people eager to achieve the recognition and privileges that now come with the first rung of elected office and who appreciate the role of BIG money in the election process.

But the unions also have a fail-safe system. Former members of the union are both educated and experienced. They are drawn toward the educational bureaucracy by greater pay, better hours or professional challenges. Pretty soon the unions and technocrats are on the same policy page and the politicians are either cooperative or forced to look for a countervailing BIG with philosophical differences to the unions to stay in office.

- How else, other than through a system that takes care of its own, do you get teacher tenure based on *longevity* alone?

- Where else do you find it so hard to actually fire an incompetent or sexually dangerous employee? Where else is it easier to warehouse employees on *paid* leave than go through a complex procedure of dismissing them?

- How else do you get nonunion charter schools to forego demonstrably *cheaper* and widely accepted *better* special education programs? Easy. Through laws sponsored by teachers' unions that *require* special education to be provided in union shop public schools *only*. And you still think lobbycratic governance is a made-up concept.

- How is it right that a recent lawsuit against the Los Angeles Unified School District for the sexual misconduct of an elementary school teacher that may or may not have been suspected by school administrators of deviant behavior resulted in a $90 million *settlement*. The superiors who ignored the potential problem are given a free ride. Worse, society suffers when every settlement dollar robs a kid of a better education.

Are you getting a feeling for what lobbycratic governance has come to and why that the public might want to expend some serious energy to reclaim control of their own government for their own benefit?

9.
CASE STUDY:
IVORY

This is an in-depth look at how lobbyists representing the animal interventionist groups, technocrats in the U.S. Fish and Wildlife Service and state-level equivalent agencies, and many mostly liberal politicians in Congress and state houses have been working to virtually end the sale and movement of objects made from or with ivory. The stated purpose of their effort is to protect elephants in Africa that are threatened with extinction at the hands of poachers seeking their tusks for East Asian markets.

I play a role with two of a number of smaller groups on the opposite side of this troika — as the Political Representative of the International Ivory Society and as Managing Director of the Ivory Education Institute. The latter organization is dedicated to improving understanding of the historical, cultural and practical uses of ivory. The IEI maintains that the problem of poaching is an African one related primarily to the adoption of managed conservation methods and the ending of a culture of corruption. Poaching needs an African solution.

The Institute also believes that the sale of ivory artifacts in the U.S. has no connection to the current plight of some elephant populations. It also believes that ivory that comes from extinct species or non-endangered animals cannot have any serious impact on the well being of elephants in Africa.

UNDERSTANDING IVORY

First, a little background on ivory. It comes from teeth that grow, for the most part, outside of an animal's mouth in the form of tusks. Tusks not only come from elephants, walruses and narwhals, but also from boars and warthogs as well as mammoths and mastodons. Ivory is also derived from the teeth of hippopotamuses and whales even though these don't protrude from the animal's mouth.

Teeth are chemically different from bones, horns, antlers, hoofs and other parts of an animal's body. Because teeth are remarkably resilient to deterioration, they have long been used to identify bodies. This same property encouraged civilizations to record elements of their history on ivory. Elephant ivory was not only known during times of the pharaohs, it is mentioned 13 times in Biblical verses. Given its longevity, special color and rarity, ivory became a favorite material for religious objects and symbols from the earliest days of the Common Era through the Renaissance.

Later its uses expanded. With the onset of the industrial revolution in Western Europe during the 1700s, a great number of newly rich entrepreneurs found themselves searching for ways to occupy their now required leisure time. It was an era that expected the wealthy to demonstrate their economic status by avoiding the need to pursue any form of daily labor. While that was hard for men of action and accomplishment, it was necessary if they were to maintain their standing on an 18th century list of most successful men.

Nearly all of these newly wealthy men lacked the great tracts of land for hunting pursuits or riding sports. They needed something else to occupy their daylight hours. Eventually they coalesced around a French game called billiards — an activity that could both keep them busy and satisfy their competitive instincts.

The particular appeal of billiards was that it involved both offensive and defensive strategies — just like croquet, another popular French game of the time. Billiards, however, was played indoors on a table far from the bothersome interference of inclement weather. Balls made from ivory, rather than the wood used for croquet balls, soon proved to have greater spring. That added enormously to the game's excitement by rewarding those willing to take the risks that a banked or ricocheted shot required.

The ivory needed for the dimensions and consistency of a billiard ball could come only from the dense top one-third of an elephant tusk. The rest of the tusk, like a human tooth, is hollow with blood vessels and nerve fibers running up the center cavity to nourish and guide the appendage. Rather than throw the rest of the tusk away as useless waste, it was coveted by artisans to make handles, tools, jewelry, devotional objects, decorations and much more. For many reasons, white gold, as ivory came to be called, was the first mass recyclable material.

In the 19th century, ivory came to have a totally different usefulness in the United States. There it became an important part of the enormously popular, space-saving upright piano. That piano helped change the cultural face of America. As the country recovered from the disruptions of the Civil War and pioneers filled in the land across the continent with growing communities, most middle-class families aspired to have one of these instruments in their parlors. An ability to play the piano soon became as important to the marriage potential of the daughters of socially important households as the skills they evidenced in cooking, sewing and conversation.

The keys on these instruments were all fashioned from ivory. It wasn't a question of aesthetics so much as practicality. The hot, humid U.S. summers not only helped keep the ivory keys lubricated — while warping the hardwood keys found on pianos and similar instruments from Europe — but it absorbed the perspiration from the fingertips of performers. Equally important, ivory's natural tackiness to the touch prevented perspiring fingers from slipping and could better highlight an individual's technique. The demand for ivory zoomed. A lot of this ivory came from the excess parts of a tusk not used for billiard balls. Some of the rest came from the tusks of animals that died of old age, disease and herd conflicts. Prior to early Victorian times, guns were not as powerful or as reliable to ensure that an elephant could be brought down in mid-charge. As a result, it is likely that a lot of older ivory objects were worked from animals that had died of natural causes.

But ivory had a vulnerability to temperature. Piano keys and billiard balls were prone to crack and split whenever temperatures changed suddenly. This occurred in mansions, chateaux and castles as well as in the more modest smaller homes across the Great Plains and Europe before central heating and air conditioning were available to stabilize indoor temperatures.

The problem of cracking and splitting inspired the development of the first artificial plastic material — celluloid. Manufactured from wood mixed with camphor oil, this man-made material offered a good substitute for ivory billiard balls and piano keys. But it also offered entrepreneurs a lot more. Its great flexibility, unusual strength and low cost inspired the creation and use of other plastic products. After World War I, plastic became the rage for a wide variety of consumer goods. Ivory in turn acquired the reputation of something old, yellowed, lined, even fusty. Plastics were fresh, bright, sleek, chic and could be adopted for a wide range of uses.

The ascendancy of plastic and the decline of ivory, continued in the United States and Europe until the late 1960s. Then, the feminist revolution as well as inflationary pressures brought women back to the workplace. But many of these women were now filling professional positions. They wanted elegant, classic jewelry pieces to maintain their femininity despite wearing masculine-looking suits and tie-like neck scarves in their offices. At the same time, they didn't want anything flashy or ostentatious.

The arbiters of fashion decreed that ivory jewelry best answered that need. It became the accessory of choice for women in the business world. Soon large numbers of elephants in Africa came under increased pressure in the rush to supply all the brooches, bracelets, earrings, pins, clasps, necklaces, brooches and other decorative items demanded by modern professional women active in the fields of finance, commerce, medicine, publishing, law and beyond.

THE EVOLVING SITUATION TODAY

This was also the era of gaining independence for most of the countries of sub-Saharan Africa. Populations were expanding and often coming up against the great game preserves that had been set aside by the colonialists to separate the wild animals from the human beings in their neighboring settlements and for hunting. Elephants, for one, demand enormous amounts of space to thrive — elephants walk 20 to 30 miles a day — and are a major destructive force of agricultural installations. The clash between humans and animals on the borders between settled communities and the protected savannahs and forests of Africa led to inevitable and significant losses among elephants.

By the 1970s many nations had recognized the possibility that the world's largest land mammal was in danger of eradication in the wild. As a result, these nations formed an international organization to oversee the protection of flora and fauna from irreversible harm. The result was passage of the Convention on International Trade in Endangered Species of Wild Fauna and Flora under the auspices of the United Nations — CITES (pronounced *SIGH-tees* in English by everyone who deals with their activities).

The convention went into force in 1975. A secretariat to develop and maintain the restrictions imposed by the treaty was formed in Geneva. Now more than 180 nations have agreed to the rules of CITES to protect elephants, rhinoceroses, tigers and other threatened animal and plant species.

That seemed to solve the immediate problem for elephants and poaching went down. Then the Chinese economy took off at the beginning of the 21st century. Many Chinese could now afford items that had been out of reach previously — cars, homes, education and objects made from or with ivory. Ivory conveyed power, wealth and beauty, and represented good fortune to most Chinese.

Millions now wanted an ivory seal, an ivory bracelet, an ivory carving or ivory chopsticks. Why, particularly, the latter? An ancient Chinese legend explains the attraction.

It was said that once upon a time an emperor had dipped his ivory chopsticks into a newly presented food dish and noticed that their tips turned color as the first bite was being raised to his mouth. He im-

mediately stopped and ordered an aide to taste the new food. After the unfortunate aide was gripped by a sudden seizure and taken from the dining hall, the story spread that the ivory chopsticks had saved the emperor from a certain and miserable death. Ivory became associated in Chinese mythology with imparting good fortune to those who own it.

There is absolutely no scientific evidence that ivory can change color so rapidly in the face of arsenic, strychnine or any other famously quick acting poison. On the contrary, modern day experiments by scientists engaged by the Ivory Education Institute have determined that it takes at least 50 to 60 minutes for ivory of any age or type to absorb sufficient moisture to bring a change of coloration to an ivory surface. But having noted that, try getting a famously superstitious people like the Chinese to believe it. Superstitions may be fairy tales, but they are still powerful factors in the thinking and actions of many people.

So demand for ivory grew in China towards the end of the first decade of the 21st century. That growth was mirrored in other East Asian countries with large populations of Chinese heritage, such as found in Thailand, Malaysia and Vietnam. In the Philippines, a strong market for such religious objects as prayer book covers, rosary beads, crosses and statutes arose.

Elephants once again came under heavy pressure from the business interests and gangs who engaged the poachers. All of this activity was greatly abetted by corrupt government authorities — from park rangers to port police to customs officials — happy to be rewarded for just being somewhere else or doing another task when illegal activities were occurring in their areas of responsibility.

AMERICAN GOVERNMENT REACTION

The first blush of renewed concern from the U.S. government arose when animal interventionist groups gained the attention of the President's staff in anticipation of an official visit to Tanzania. There in 2013, President Obama announced an initiative to support Tanzanian efforts to combat poaching.

The U.S. Fish and Wildlife Service, the designated agent of the U.S. government to support and enforce CITES policies, issued Director's Order Number 210 to provide guidance to U.S. officials on how to tighten loopholes to prevent the importation or marketing of illegal ivory — ivory without proper documentation to establish its provenance. Never mind that there wasn't much coming into the United States that anyone could identify except for an isolated case here and there, the Order did offer positive proof to animal interventionist groups of America's official concern for elephants.

Later, a number of collector organizations protested this public relations exercise, noting that the Order had *not* been subjected to public comment. Had it, many groups said, the lack of evidence to support the premise that the U.S. was a hotbed for illegal ivory sales would certainly have been challenged. This, of course, was not by accident. It is another good example of how lobbycratic governance works today. Favored lobbyists working with sympathetic technocrats do as much by administrative fiat as possible — and as little by legislation as the lawyers determine is defensible — in order to be able to control the direction and impact of public policy. That may be changing. A U.S. District judge found in June 2016 that the Obama administration had been wrong in issuing rules on hydraulic fracturing in light of a direct Congressional prohibition on such matters. A number of other suits on executive orders overreaching legislative boundaries are pending.

But carping about the questionable legality of Director's Order 210 became moot when lobbyists representing the animal interventionist groups prevailed on the U.S. Fish and Wildlife technocrats to issue a set of proposed changes to Rule 4(d) of the Endangered Species Act governing African elephants. Because the issuance of Rule 4(d) had followed the proper procedures, any changes made to it would have to duplicate that process.

These administrative rules are crafted by lobbyists and technocrats with input from a phalanx of private and government lawyers. Public comment is kept at a minimum even though the formal rules implementing a law go through a lengthy comment period and prescribed review process. But once modified and if eventually approved for publication in the *Federal Register*, they have the same force as any law passed by Congress and signed by the President. It is definitely not your father's government.

Because of the proposed changes affecting ivory ownership and trade envisioned by Rule 4(d), it was strongly opposed by groups who questioned a number of its assumptions. Here, in part, is the Ivory Education Institute's official submission to the Fish and Wildlife Service on aspects of the proposed rule change. Even though the comments were ignored, they are presented here as an example of how law is formulated by the technocrats in the era of lobbycratic governance.

> *The U.S. Fish and Wildlife Service states that the proposed changes to Rule 4(d) would "increase protection for African elephants" and would update "measures that are appropriate for the current conservation needs of the species." These two assertions by the U.S. government are a denial of basic economic law and [reflect] an arrogant belief that the U.S. knows better than local officials how best to conserve African wildlife.*

> - *By further restricting ownership of ivory in the United States without dealing with East Asian demand for ivory, it is likely that the U.S. government will duplicate its achievements during Prohibition: Failure to deal with demand then only fueled increased alcohol consumption. The same problem has doomed the efforts to stem the flow of illicit drugs[†] and stop illegal immigrants into the country.*

> - *Moreover, restricting the availability of ivory, while leaving demand for ivory unchanged, can only increase the price of raw ivory in the market-*

[†]*The Guardian* said this at the time of the IEI comment: "By any standard, the global war on drugs has been an abject failure . . ."

place. The laws of economics cannot be repealed by administrative edict. By restricting supply while ignoring demand, the USFWS makes the rewards for poaching more attractive and the danger to elephants . . . even greater.

- *In addition, by assuming that U.S. domestic programs will provide better protection for African elephants — without a by-your-leave to the countries in question and without acknowledging that hundreds of African communities have a major stake in the well-being of their wildlife — the U.S. adopts a posture that reflects the worst of the colonial era. If the U.S. truly wants to help African elephants, the USFWS and the non-governmental organizations ought to suspend their expensive propaganda efforts involving PR events and advertising campaigns (aimed at the people of the United States) and spend those resources where they will do the most good [for elephants] in Africa.*

- *Promoting restrictions on American ownership of ivory objects that were brought into the U.S. legally will have NO demonstrable impact on elephant herds in Africa and will do great harm to America's cultural heritage in years to come. Making some accommodation for "antiques" reflects an old-fashioned, outmoded, and questionable understanding of what constitutes an artifact worth preserving and protecting.*

The definition of antique used by the U.S. government turns out to have no relationship to cultural norms. The 100-year standard arises as an accident of the calendar. The drafters of the 1930 Smoot-Hawley Tariff Act found that mass-produced manufactured products first outnumbered handcrafted objects in 1830. The 100-year rule to qualify an object as an "antique" has since been based on this informal economic assessment, not a cultural determination. To continue to use the 100-year standard shuts out the cultural treasures created during the Art Deco period of the 1930s as well as the post-World War II era and ignores cultural recognition for such important technological advances and design developments as the automobile, computer, Internet and mobile phone.[†]

ANTI-IVORY OPPOSITION

To provide justification for the claim that the U.S. is awash in illegal ivory, the Natural Resources Defense Council commissioned a study of the amount of ivory in the American commercial marketplace.

The 2014 study, by Dr. Daniel Stiles, consisted of a survey of ivory objects on sale in Los Angeles and San Francisco. Dr. Stiles pointedly refused to identify any of the ivory he saw on sale as patently illegal. In fact, Stiles was charged by NDRC

[†]Amendments to Rule 4(d) governing ivory were eventually adopted and published in the *Federal Register* and went into effect on July 6, 2016. Collectors soon transferred their concerns to enforcement of the new rules. Doug Ritter, the experienced head of the Knife Rights Foundation, noted this in an email: ". . . government enforcement is not to be trusted and is subject entirely to the whims of the enforcement folks at every level. It takes little to shift to a strict and harsh enforcement stance by leadership. Nobody cares what the initial 'intentions' were."

only with determining whether any ivory he saw could "possibly" have been worked after 1977. The author accompanied Stiles during his visit to an antique fair in Santa Monica, California. Nearly every piece seen that day could have easily been categorized as "possibly" illegal. Stiles subsequently and significantly noted that only a few pieces were "probably" worked in the post-1977 period.[†]

For an agency of the U.S. government to misuse data from a private sector study is typical of the methods of lobbycratic governance. Agencies and interest groups work together to fashion desired answers to a public policy questions and once a study is completed and a report distributed, they selectively quote from it, often ignoring significant facts, to justify their positions. This kind of tactic, in our view, is tantamount to fraud.

Put simply, California is not flooded with illegal ivory, the Stiles study did not change that fact, and the USFWS was well aware of this. But without an independent legislature questioning witnesses in open hearings and creating a public record of the proceedings, there is nothing to offset how lobbyists and technocrats collude to achieve policy posi-

---

[†]Stiles went further in his submission on changes to Rule 4(d). He said that the USFWS intentionally misused his data in this statement: "Stiles estimated, in his 2014 follow-up study, that as much as one-half of the ivory for sale in two California cities during his survey had been imported *illegally*. (Emphasis added.) All of this demonstrates the need to impose restrictions on commercializing elephant ivory within the United States." Stiles responded tartly: "The report in question said nothing about 'imported illegally.'" The Service, typically, ignored the rebuke.

tions the organizations want and the technocrats provide. It may be a "legally" achieved result, but it is no less a fraud on the body politic.

MANIPULATING FACTS

A government of, by and for the people is one where elected representatives are entrusted with making the rules that affect everyone's lives and well being. When that duty is abrogated, as is now being done in the United States, the void is filled by lobbyists and technocrats.

> **The simple truth is that the lobbyists can offer an array of incentives to both technocrats and legislators to obtain the policy ends their organizations desire. The only counterveiling force in an era of lobbycratic governance is another interest group with equal resources and a different policy objective.**

One of the hocus pocus tricks of the symbiotic relationship between lobbyists and technocrats is to quote statistics that "look" supportive of a desired point but don't always buttress the eventual conclusion. Take these examples on the issue of ivory:

- The U.S. authorities claim that between 1996 and 2012 there were 14,070 "separate raw or worked ivory seizures in 72 countries and territories." Big numbers, bad impression. But those numbers actually indicate that over *17* years(!) there were an average of only 828 seizures per year among the *72* countries. That amounts to just 11 to 12 seizures per country

213

per year! Is this evidence of an epidemic or a slick drafting trick to try to shock the conscience of the reader predisposed to the point of view?

- In another instance, the U.S. Fish and Wildlife Service notes that CITES states that 25,000 elephants were illegally killed in 2011 and 22,000 in 2012. But the *decrease* of more than 10 percent a year, statistically significant in any other context, is left un-remarked by the Service. The technique is startling. The Service presents facts — so as not to be accused of hiding derogatory information — but then ignores them because they do not comport with the claim of an "alarming rise in poaching of the species." Technocrats in government, at the least, should be punctiliously honest. Unfortunately, they are not.

- Here is a third example of the shady way a government agency has employed statistics: At page 45157 of the *Federal Register*, Volume 80, No. 145 for Wednesday, July 29, 2015, the Service states that there were "12,073 ... elephant carcasses found between 2002 and the end of 2013 at 53 MIKE [Monitoring the Illegal Killing of Elephants] sites in 29 countries across Africa." A casual reading of that statement might elicit shock and revulsion at the total death count. That seems to be the desired effect of the Fish and Wildlife Service, because an analysis of the data suggests that over the *12* years involved, only about 1,000 elephants died per year or 35 per country.

That is but a tiny fraction of the *35,000* that most animal interventionists groups claim are killed each year. Many could have died from natural causes or as a source of bush food for local inhabitants. They are hardly indicative of "fuel [for] the growing illegal trade in ivory."

But without offering any analysis, the animal interventionist groups and the Service use these kinds of numbers to burden the 13 million American citizens believed to own millions of different ivory objects acquired *legally* with stringent new restrictions.

The *Federal Register* also permits a variation of the lawyer's trick of data dumps. These give the appearance of having tons of supporting evidence for a position but don't bother to go beyond an avalanche of citations to support the Service's position of an "increase in poaching of elephants and the escalation of the illegal trade in ivory."[†]

Anyone who has taught at the university level recognizes the technique: The larger the smoke

---

[†]That statement at page 45156(c) of the *Federal Register*, Volume 80, No. 145 for Wednesday, July 29, 2015, is then followed by this thoroughly opaque note: "[See] documents made available at CoP16. See, in particular, CoP16 Doc. 53.1, Monitoring the illegal killing of elephants (including the Addendum); CoP16 Doc. 53.2.2, Monitoring of illegal trade in ivory and other elephant specimens; and Elephants in the Dust—the African Elephant Crisis, all available at http://www.cites.org. Status of African elephant populations and levels of illegal killing and the illegal trade in ivory: A report to the African Elephant Summit, December

screen, the harder it is to determine where scholarship ends and the appearance of research begins. Do these referenced documents actually support the USFWS position in their entirety? Is there an effort here to dazzle readers with the agency's "thoroughness," knowing full well that few if any individuals or groups in opposition to the USFWS position will have all the referenced documents at hand or the resources to review each of the citations for its relevance?

Why are no tables, highlights or summaries of these documents included? Maybe some of the data is as non-supportable of the Fish and Wildlife position as other material it submitted. Perhaps the Service didn't have room for this type of additional documentation? Hardly. The proposed changes to Rule 4(d) covers more than 90 three-column pages of nine-point type in the *Federal Register*. No effort evidenced to save trees here.

It is just one more example of technocrats retreating to a position where it wants the public to adopt a "trust us" attitude. It is as if they are offended at the thought that the public does not automati-

---

2013 (also available at http://www.cites.org) provides an update to information presented at CoP16. A further update on the status of African elephants was prepared for the 65th meeting of the CITES Standing Committee (SC65), in July 2014, and presented in Annex 1 to document SC65 Doc. 42.1, Elephant conservation, illegal killing and ivory trade. CoP16 Doc. 53.1 and its Addendum (prepared by the CITES Secretariat), the December 2013 report for the African Elephant Summit . . . " Similar citations and references to other documents continued on the following page.

cally accept what they do as impartial, fair and just. Most technocrats understand that there are Federal officials who have taken bribes, looked the other way in enforcement matters or done a favor for a friend of relative. Nearly all technocrats just can't accept that someone might think *they* would engage in that kind of behavior. *They*, after all, are sworn to uphold the laws of the land and would never do anything that violates the Constitution or put ordinary citizens at risk. Except when they do.

Technocrats claim their educational credentials as reason alone to trust their judgment and probity:

> **About 22 percent of all federal workers have graduate degrees compared to 10 percent in the private sector. A trend in the federal workforce is moving towards bringing on even more highly educated personnel: 93 percent of new hires between 2004-2012 had at least a bachelor's degree and there was a 56 percent increase of employees with a master's or professional degree.**

And if you trust a federal employee to do the "right" thing because they are better educated than the general population, then write a check to the next person who offers you an interest in the tolls being collected on a new bridge across New York's East River. The only thing education and ethics have in common is an initial letter of "e."

Of course, the attack on ivory is not the only place where citizens feel that the U.S. government is using spurious statistics to overstep its legitimate role in a democratic society. A high profile case in

2016 involved cell phone privacy. The FBI asked a federal court to force Apple Inc. to help in unlocking data that might be stored on an iPhone. Apple refused on grounds that the intrusion might compromise the privacy of all iPhone users. The Justice Department lawyers dismissed this argument with its own 11th grade interpretation of how the U.S. government works in an official court filing: "The courts, the executive branch and Congress — not Apple — share the power to decide how best to balance public safety and privacy."[†] Right. And the Attorney General is totally unaware of the role that monied groups and their technocratic allies play in the actual conduct of American governance.

Of course, when the policy shoe is on the other foot, the U.S. government is happy to defy the rule of law. In the days of the George W. Bush administration, the U.S. said it would not enforce the Kyoto Protocols. It didn't, despite this kind of editorial reaction in the *Los Angeles Times*:

> *The thought that the United States would not begin a process of curbing its carbon dioxide and other global warming emissions — claiming to do so might put people out of work, do other harm to the U.S. economy, and exacerbate the U.S. energy crisis — makes us look arrogant, selfish, and incredibly shortsighted to the rest of the world.*

[†]In June 2016, *The New York Times* shamelessly called Donald Trump's reference to a "rigged" legal system "a threat to America's carefully balanced political system." This, despite the newspaper's almost daily reports on how the three branches abuse and ignore each other.

218

When the federal effort to ban ivory bogged down, the animal interventionist groups pushed for a state by state ban. California obliged by passing Assembly Bill 96. Almost immediately, the Ivory Education Institute asked the Superior Court of Los Angeles to prohibit its implementation. The IEI feared the real harm this state law could do to collectors and the culture. The Institute based its position on the fact that the law was likely unconstitutional:

> **It involves taking of property without due process of law and it is a prohibited *ex post facto* statute, in that it declared an ivory object illegal to sell after it had been legitimately purchased [and without any restrictions on its eventual disposition].**

At the outset, the Ivory Education Institute, was battling the State of California, a formidable enough opponent. But five of the biggest animal interventionist groups —the Natural Resources Defense Council, the Center for Biological Diversity, the Humane Society of the United States, the International Fund for Animal Welfare and the Wildlife Conservation Society — apparently didn't think so. After all, AB 96 was *their* bill from the outset and they felt they had as much right to defend it from attack as the State of California.[†]

[†]The law was written and presented to the Speaker of the Assembly. But it took lobbycratic governance a step beyond the federal model. The Fish and Wildlife Department was

The five organizations — calling themselves the Conservation Groups — clearly hate the thought of being left outside of the tent while all the action on the ivory issue is going on inside. What better way to show the 300,000 members of the NRDC that the organization is doing something while at the same time using the self-generated costs of defending the lawsuit as the basis to appeal for more funds to support their other activities?

The ivory issue in California seems a microcosm of how lobbycratic governance works. AB 96 was written by lobbyists without bothering with government technocrats. Elected officials were mostly cheer leaders and facilitators in getting it voted and signed into law in return for potential campaign support. Harsh? Not really. Ask any California legislator to explain exactly what AB 96 will accomplish for the *people* of California. Ask them how *specifically* the law will protect elephants in Africa. And given the federal government's overwhelming responsibility for matters of foreign policy, what right do these interventionist groups have to use California's resources to project an independent foreign policy toward Africa?

---

not even involved. In fact, officials of the agency told the author they opposed AB 96. Never mind. The Speaker's power in the legislature to control the destiny of all legislation made the bill law. The ownership of these groups was laid bare in a June 2016 court filing in which they "intervened as defendants." The State of California is the defendant; they are merely official "observers," but the nicety of the distinction is lost on them.

10.
CHANGING THE LOBBYCRATIC STATE

One of my pet peeves is reading an erudite article in a newspaper or magazine that analyzes some current issue, looming problem or pending situation, but never gets around to suggesting any specific steps to prevent the problem, resolve the issue or deal with the situation.[†] It is as if the authors are afraid to offer any form of solution lest they eventually prove inappropriate, unnecessary or wrong. They seem to be afraid of losing their guru status

---

[†]Dow Chemical, in a 2012 Fortune Magazine advertisement, created a word to capture the company's approach toward problems its people encounter. The company said it was involved in "Solutionism — the New Optimism." Dow declared *solutionism* as an attitude. It is something that most media pundits avoid but something we can thoroughly endorse to change lobbycratic governance into something better.

and jeopardizing future assignments to write other erudite pieces that validate their relevance and keep them in the public policy loop, even if they have no fresh ideas to offer.

Sometimes a thorough analysis of a problem leads to a simple solution — the type that "experts" are loathe to mention lest it somehow devalue their erudition and exalted status. The following story making the rounds of the Internet in the 2016 campaign season is illustrative of this point.

> *Once upon a time there was a king who wanted to go fishing. He called on the royal weather forecaster and the weatherman assured him that he didn't see much chance of rain that day.*
>
> *On the way to the river he met a farmer. The farmer said: "Your Majesty, you should return to the palace because in a short time a downpour is going to engulf this area."*
>
> *The king replied: "I hold the palace meteorologist in high regard. He is an expert — extensively educated and superbly trained. And besides, I pay him a very high wage. He gave me a different forecast." So the king continued on his way.*
>
> *A short time later a torrential rain fell from the sky. The king was totally soaked and his entourage were saddened by his shameful condition and spoiled plans. Furious, the king returned to the palace and fired the meteorologist. Then he summoned the farmer and offered him the prestigious and high paying role of royal forecaster.*
>
> *The farmer said, "Your Majesty, I know nothing*

about forecasting. I obtain my information from my donkey. If I see my donkey's ears drooping, it means with certainty that it will rain."

So the king bought the donkey. Thus began the practice of hiring dumb asses to work in government and occupy its highest paid and most influential positions. And the practice has not changed to this day.

The tendency of "experts" to draw conclusions that cover all contingencies is not going to happen here. Having examined how lobbyists and technocrats guided by lawyers and abetted by politicians have come to dominate the mechanisms of government that control the business of the United States, it is time to explore the means for changing the direction, control and operation of that government — to reassert the intended role of a government that is of, by and for the people.

PROPOSITION 13

Lest some think that the task of taking back control of government is beyond the possible for ordinary citizens, consider Proposition 13 in California — a proposed 1978 amendment to the state constitution that was opposed by every major political poobah at the time. It passed by a narrow margin that November and remains a force today in California governance. Proposition 13 came on the scene because local politicians of the day did nothing to stem the relentless rising taxes on real and personal property to meet whatever demand was made of them for increased government support. While the politicians of both parties thought that real estate owners could simply raise their rents to cover the increased tax payments, they didn't reckon with millions of older homeowners who weren't in the real estate market. They were living in their homes and living on fixed incomes.

A lot of these people had to stretch their limited funds to meet the rising costs of medicines, food and transportation. The possibility that many of them could be forced out of their homes after 30 or more years because they couldn't meet the ever-increasing tax assessments filled them with fear. The politicians, pandering to one powerful intere-est group or another, ignored them. Oldsters were not organized. Then two men came along — Howard Jarvis and Paul Gann — to channel the anger. Jarvis, a political activist of the day, told them they *could* do something about the property taxes that were starting to eat them alive.

Put simply, Proposition 13 mandated a fixed property tax rate of 1 percent of the then current assessed value with annual increases of no more than 2 percent. Period. It was simple, clean, definitive. The market value of properties could only be recognized for tax assessments only at the time of reconstruction or sale. Punto!

Technocrats and their lawyers were appalled that anyone would dare make a law without any of the ifs, ands, buts and wherefores that were their life blood. Politicians were stunned. Their candy store was being robbed before their eyes and they would be left with no easy way to provide the funds to take care of the increased services that their favorite constituents demanded. No one suggested they could say no to these requests for ever more funds. The issue was so important to the well being of technocrats and politicians that they pushed the U.S. Supreme Court to answer a fundamental Proposition 13 question: Did the disparity between the taxes paid by two side-by-side residents — one a long time homeowner and the other new to the neighborhood — violate the equal protection clause of the 14th Amendment to the U.S. Constitution. The court said no in *Nordlinger v. Hahn*.

Proposition 13 — the People's Initiative to Limit Property Taxation — made a huge difference. It ended the idea that any source of taxes is a giant piggy bank for technocrats and politicians to use as needed. It also locked into the California constitution a requirement that any subsequent change in any tax had to be approved by two-thirds of the legislature or the people.[†]

California took a long time to adjust to the changes wrought by Proposition 13; in many ways it is still adjusting its expectations and its methods of raising public revenues to the limitations that Proposition 13 has imposed. It is also important to note that the

---

[†]The president of the Howard Jarvis Taxpayers Association — the watchdog interest group that has protected Proposition 13 from various efforts to reduce its effect — wrote in the *Los Angeles Daily News* in April 2016 that ". . . political elites hate voter approval" because it is so often withheld. To obviate public involvement, the technocrats, their investment advisors and their lawyers have invented ". . . new esoteric debt instruments like 'certificates of participation' and 'revenue bonds. . .'" that do not require voter approval.

measure initiated "taxpayer revolts" in other parts of the country and is said to have contributed to the election of Ronald Reagan as President in 1980. But most of all, Proposition 13 reminded everyone that governments in the United States belong to their citizens, not to technocrats and politicians who are meant to work for them.

The lesson of Proposition 13 (and Brexit — the June 2016 vote in the United Kingdom to extricate the country from the control of European Union technocrats) needs to be heeded. When citizens choose to use the ballot box to change the way government deals with problems, it is much more effective than:

- Letters to editors
- Email chains
- Internet petitions
- Marches
- Rallies
- Boycotts
- Sanctions
- Riots

These are nice for TV, chat radio and Internet blogs, but not for real change. There is no reason to believe that the American people cannot summon the will that produced Proposition 13 and Brexit to change the way the *United States* government is run. For starters, they need to sharpen their strongest weapon under our current system — voting — to get the changes that are required.

The NAACP has called voting a "civil sacrament" — the one act that symbolizes a person's commitment to his community and participation in society. It is the single strongest weapon available to American citizens to peacefully alter the direction of their country, but one used less and less as the people become more and more doubtful of its usefulness or resigned to the control the nation's political elite exercise. The *Los Angeles Times* refers to this as the "disengagement" — the belief that "there is little of importance that an election can change." Those who do vote are angry that "political parties and big money donors have tried to limit their choice of candidates or preordained election outcomes."

Worse, while many citizens are turned off by voting, some states are moving to *restrict* voting even further:

- States such as Kansas, Georgia and Alabama have insisted on picture identification cards to prevent registration "fraud" even though none has ever been demonstrated. As a result, the restriction is viewed by many as a way to prevent minorities and poor people — many of whom lack the type of credentials (driver's license, passport) — required.

- The machinery to conduct elections is obsolete in many jurisdictions — highlighted by the hanging and pregnant chads that remained attached to punch card ballots in Florida in the 2000 Presidential election. Those ambiguous votes were reviewed to see if a voter's "intentions" could be discerned. They had a major bearing on the total counted as cast for electors pledged to Governor George W. Bush or Vice President Al Gore. Recall that only 537 popular votes separated the two in Florida at the end of the recount and eventually became the margin of Mr. Bush's Florida — and national victory. Upgrading voting technology across the country might cost as much as $1 billion if all of the precincts —last counted at some 185,000 — simultaneously received the same type and quality of equipment.

- Another tactic to restrict voting was employed in Maricopa County (Phoenix) in the 2016 Arizona Presidential primary. Citing budgetary problems, the number of voting precincts available to accommodate voters was slashed from 200 in 2012 to 60. That meant long lines long into the night, which had the intended effect. Many voters gave up in despair or needed to tend to other responsibilities without completing a ballot.

All of this maneuvering to manipulate the end result of an election shows a distrust of the average citizen to make a reasonable choice. This changes radically if voting in the United States were to be made *mandatory* and registration requirements were to become uniform across the country. It could restore voting to a preeminent position in the control that the public exercises over its government.

At last count, some 22 countries have mandatory voting requirements. Many of them are responsible democracies such as Argentina, Australia, Belgium and Mexico; some are newer to practicing real democracy such as Brazil, Ecuador and Nauru; and some are authoritarian regimes that use voting as a means of control as in Singapore and North Korea. All seem to view voting as a way to reinforce the requirements of citizenship. All enforce the requirement with various penalties for those who fail to vote.

Take Peru. It has required citizens between the ages of 18 and 70 to vote in all elections since 1933. (Older citizens may choose to vote or not without penalty; citizens who have religious objections to voting or an abhorrence to all the candidates are allowed to cast an empty ballot or vote "en blanco.") Citizens are not only required to vote, they are also required to act as election judges at polling stations. Failure to vote or refusal to serve results in a fine.

The amount of the fine for not voting depends on one's economic condition. Poor people pay less for failing to vote than rich people, but both pay the same amount for not serving as an election official. The determination of one's ability to pay rests on the economic strength of the district in which a person lives, not the level of an individual's income.

If Peruvians fail to pay the non-voting fine, they lose the ability to obtain a valid, up-to-date identification card or DNI *(Documento Nacional de Identificación)*. The identification card gives Peruvians access to a host of government and non-government functions. Without a current DNI, most citizens of Peru would be unable to obtain such government services as changing an address on official records, requesting a consular function, securing a building permit, obtaining medical services, travelling abroad, registering a child for school, and so on. Even the simple act of cashing a check requires an up-to-date identification card!

If asked, most Peruvians accept the requirement of mandatory voting. They also accept the restrictions that Peruvian electoral law mandates. The country is dry for the final eight hours before an election day and the first eight hours after election day. All electioneering stops and all public places close 24 hours before election day to allow voters the space to make up their own minds. The habit of voting in each election appears to have carried over to Peruvians who have become U.S. citizens. They are active participants in the American electoral process. The same cannot be said for other immigrant communities. The journal *Democracy* notes:

> *In 2008, [the] turnout among the native-born voting-age population was 64.4 percent and only 54 percent among naturalized voting-age Americans. The disparity in turnout between native and naturalized Americans has been persistent; in 2006, naturalized citizens voted at a rate 12 percentage points lower than their native counterparts—49 percent versus 37 percent—and in 2004, there was an 11 point gap.*

The fact that Americans celebrate their freedoms by making voting *voluntary* seems to be a path that can eventually lead to the end of all freedoms. The non-voting record of newly minted citizens is particularly troubling. We have to change attitudes. In addition to insisting on a basic understanding of American history and governmental practices in our citizenship instruction in schools and outside classes, we should instill a feeling of what it means to be a citizen of the United States, an appreciation of the obligations to the community that comes with citizenship.

Many will oppose mandatory voting. Voting, they say, has always been voluntary; it ought to remain so. After all, they claim if someone can't be bothered to vote it means he or she can't be bothered to study the issues or choose among the candidates. Better that they don't vote — leave matters to those who *do* care and who *do* take the time to involve themselves in the issues. What if they are Jehovah's Witnesses and their religious principles prohibit them from active participation in such civic duties as voting? Could you, in fairness, punish these people for not voting? That sounds like something the Communist governments did after World War II. It isn't worthy of a democratic society.

Do those opposed to mandatory voting have a point or are the vast majority just putting up a smoke screen to increase their relative power and hold on the status quo? I think it is a smoke screen. Note this: Many other activities that define our society and do not alter the full exercise of our freedoms have been made *mandatory*. People may chafe at the requirements from time to time, but they either follow the law and comply or become subject to fines and penalties. If they don't, they do without something of value.

All of the following governmental requirements demand mandatory compliance. These make you think that adding voting to the list may not be such a hardship:

- Paying taxes
- Serving on juries
- Answering census questions
- Obeying the commands of a police officer
- Responding to a judge's directions
- Getting a driver's license
- Having medical insurance
- Registering for the Selective Service
- Attending school
- Being vaccinated

Participation in the voting process is certainly not as onerous as paying taxes, qualifying for a driver's license, or getting a shot, so why the resistance? Some argue that it takes too much time. Really? Voting takes more time than the paperwork to complete federal, state and local tax forms or to practice before taking the tests to earn the right to drive?

Others argue that there are no good choices on election day. Why should people be forced to decide among a bunch of losing options? Our answer to that is they wouldn't have to. Those who favor mandatory voting have no problem if millions of citizens — including those with religious objections — were to refuse to select a candidate or decide an issue. These individuals could have left the box beside the name or issue *blank*. Voting "None of the above" — as Nevadans do — or "Uncommitted" — as Connecticut permits its citizens to do

— makes a powerful statement that government cannot ignore.

Citizens who participate by not making a definite choice among the names or issues on a ballot *are* in fact making a conscious decision. Counting up the *nota* and *uncommitted* votes has a baring on the direction that government takes. Political forces are disposed to try to make the changes that will bring the dissatisfied into the political process on their side to win in the future.

What is not acceptable, in a democracy struggling to keep control of the mechanisms of government, is retreating into selfishness where *not* participating is considered acceptable, where individuals worry more about their personal lives and economic ambitions than they do about the larger community that nourishes and protects that life and their earning power.

VOTING SYSTEMS

Who votes and who doesn't has been one of the constant refrains in 2016. Newscasters and their hired guns among the statistical set were continually analyzing the entry interviews in the caucus states and the exit polls in the primary states to determine how this religious group or that, this age group or that, this income group or that, looked at the candidates and issues compared to what they told polling firms.

A theme heard over and over again is that if the country could change the *system* of voting — to get more people eligible and make it easier for everyone to vote — government would have to be more responsive to the will of the people. I am not so sure. Even tinkering with how or when a convicted felon's voting rights should be restored, if more mentally incapacitated individuals should vote, and even if non-citizens should become voters in special local elections involving school governance probably wouldn't change much. It is playing at the fringes. Getting more people to vote does not guarantee that the technocrats will rearrange their prejudices or pay closer attention to the will of the people. Getting *all* the people to vote is a different story. That results in a statement.

A few of the many changes suggested in the way we vote have been put in place by some jurisdictions; others are pending adoption. Perhaps the most controversial such change was a move by conservatives to design districts based on the number of *eligible* voters living within its boundaries rather than on the *total* population living there. The Supreme Court resoundingly reaffirmed the one person, one vote standard in 2016 by saying that districts must always be built on the basis of the *total* population.

Here are other changes in voting technology that have been advocated:

- Make bi-annual national election days a holiday as it is in many countries.

- Create election weekends, instead of a single day, to give everyone more opportunities to vote.

- Do all voting by mail.

- Hold elections on Sundays when more people are off work.

- Do voting on the Internet.

- Allow ballots to carry more information about candidates and issues.

- Provide single-use Internet services at bus stops, coffee shops, grocery stores and gas stations — anywhere people go regularly and in large numbers — through portable devices connected through a Wi-Fi network.

- Provide registration up to and including the day of election.

- Tie registration to college enrollment, driver's license renewals, utility payments or some other painless, routine activity to accommodate those who move in the 30 days before an election as well as those who tend to procrastinate until the last moment.

- Eliminate registration altogether.[†]

What is left out of all of these erudite and imaginative ways to increase voter participation is the obvi-

---

[†]Registration will probably be a requirement if we want to be represented by those who live near us. Getting people registered would be required if voting is made mandatory so privileges can be awarded. In the 1992 presidential election, 4.2 million Latinos voted; by 2012 the number nearly tripled to 11.2 million. Another 3.2 million Latino kids and 1.2 million newly minted Latino citizens will be eligible to vote in 2016. Will they get registered? History is not on their side: Only 58 percent are registered to vote compared with 75 percent in both the white and black communities.

ous conclusion that voting is a chore. It certainly is, but the focus of the smart money, as seen by all the bright ideas above, is on the final requirements of the task, not on the tough part in the *middle* between registration and voting — making the choices.

In my experience with various campaigns and after doing a special analysis on an election in San Bernardino, California, it became clear that most voters make up their minds at *random* instances during a campaign. No one is sure when the light goes on or what triggers the moment when a voter decides to lift the window shade to pay sufficient attention to make up his or her mind on the candidates or issues. It could be an article read, a chance remark in a conversation, a billboard seen, a mailing piece received, something encountered on the Internet. But once the voter is ready to receive all the information available on candidates or issues, the assessment is swift and sure. He or she listens, considers, decides. Boom. Once the mind has been made up, the window shade lowers and the only election information to penetrate from that point on reinforces the decision made, but does not change it.

Interviews have also found that most of those who don't vote see voting as a duplication of their high school misery — the tests they dreaded but couldn't avoid and on which they needed a reasonable grade to be sure of eventual graduation. For a lot of people, voting appears to be a "test" on a subject most people hated in high school — civics.

No wonder. Most classes in government involve remembering facts that will have absolutely no bearing on their future or their lives. How many of us really need to remember the number of elected representatives in the House of Representatives, the reason for the difference in terms between a senator and a representative, how a pocket veto differs from a formal veto, and so on.

Worse, when voting is seen as a test, it suggests that individuals have to study the differences in candidates and causes in order to "pass." Soon these voters learn that all elections are about choices and each choice involves conflict and no shortage of confusion. The result is that voters end up in some kind of agony trying to decide whom to vote for or how to decide an issue on the ballot. Then they figure out that they don't have to take *this* "test." Playing hookey from an election has no penalty, no punishment, no consequences. Wow! Is this a great country or what?

In the end millions of American citizens take the easy way out of their civic responsibility and avoid the polls. In some jurisdictions, these citizens learn that there is an added bonus in not voting. If you aren't registered to vote, you may not be "seen" by the computers searching for citizens to serve on juries. The film, "Swing Vote," with Kevin Costner, makes that point very clearly.

Our view is that all of the "end game" suggestions to increase voting may help at the margins, but won't likely change the current tendency for government to be controlled by technocrats, lobbyists and lawyers.

The key to increasing public participation

in elections to the point of making a real difference in governance is to have everyone vote. That could overwhelm the lobbying organizations that target handfuls of elaborately profiled citizens who will make the difference in the numbers needed to win in specific voting districts.[†]

If voting were mandatory, what kind of penalties might be imposed for failure to cast a ballot? *None,* if we had our way. We do not advocate *penalties.* Instead, we would propose giving voters *privileges* that non-voters could not enjoy until the next local, statewide or national election. Allow those who voted in the last federal, state or local election to have any one or all of the following privileges:

- Send any piece of mail to a government agency free of postage with that agency reimbursing the Postal Service. Yes, taxpayers would ultimately foot the bill, but non-voters would pay twice: In their taxes and again in the stamps they would have to buy or in the cost of hand delivery.

[†]Sometimes the simplest solutions — such as mandatory voting — turns out to also be the most elegant in a political setting. T*he Wall Street Journal* reported in April 2016 that in a town near Mumbai, India, officials decreed that anyone *not* paying taxes would receive a visit from a drum corps. When the drummers showed up at a real estate developer's house, "neighbors leaned out windows and gawked. Within hours, a red-faced Prahul Sawant had written a $945 check to settle [the] arrears [and stop the noise.]" Shaming has also worked by using Internet postings, newspaper advertising and "wanted" posters at City Hall.

- Voters would move to the front of government lines, bumping non-voters or leaving them with the least desirable slots in the day.

- Give voters direct telephone lines to get questions answered at all agencies more quickly.

- Provide voters with a special code designation that moves their emails to the top of an agency's in-box or faxes to the pile that needs priority responses.

- Provide a 25 percent discount on whatever fees and fines are demanded by a government jurisdiction. The fee could apply to a building permit, a parking ticket, a museum admission or a library fine.

- Take a 5 percent discount on all taxes due from a jurisdiction and on all court filing costs.

- Give voters free service of process in small claims legal matters in lieu of marshall fees.

- Allow voters free photocopying at libraries and government offices.

- Create voter doors for entry to government building and special voter lanes in U.S. citizen queues at all ports of entry.

- Permit previous voters to be dealt with ahead of all others except first time voters at polling stations.

Some will say that any or all of these privileges will be hard to police. Two responses to that. All ballots come with a stub that would identify voters to public officials; all voters are required to identify themselves before they cast a secret ballot. Those names could be accessed on a computer program to verify that the person had indeed gone to the polls. Would it be 100 percent foolproof? Probably not, but what is in today's world? Would some people cheat? Certainly. But none of these objections is sufficiently compelling to reject the _concept_ of providing privileges as a reward for voting.

INITIATIVES

Politics in California's capital were so uniformly corrupt at the turn of the 20th century that Governor Hiram Johnson sponsored amendments to the state's constitution to give the people the mechanisms to engage in direct democracy. He reasoned that if the legislature was not being responsive to the people, then the people themselves ought to be able to do what their elected representatives wouldn't. Johnson's three direct democracy tools have been employed for more than 100 years.

- *Initiative.* Although the rules of eligibility have been tinkered with dozens of times, the initiative is a process that allows any eligible voter to propose a constitutional amendment, law or bond issue for adoption by the people. If approved by the voters, an initiative proposition has all the force and effect of a law passed by the legislature and signed by the governor. Since its inception in California, some 1,800 initiatives have appeared on the ballot, with 123 of them approved including such landmark measures as the abolition of the poll tax (1914), limitation on taxation

(1978), and the establishment of an independent redistricting commission (2008).

- *Referendum.* Although used less than the initiative process, a referendum is the public's chance to challenge any approved law that it thinks is contrary to their interests, unconstitutional on its face, or questionable as to its effect. If the public votes to repeal the law challenged in a referendum, it becomes null and void there and then.

- *Recall.* This is the public's right to remove an office holder that it feels has done something wrong, illegal or contrary to the public's best interests. Usually, recall votes are accompanied by a simultaneous, but separate, election for a replacement office holder should the recall itself be approved and an elected official be removed in the process.

This is direct democracy at its most effective. The problem is that all three mechanisms have been hijacked by interest groups looking for a faster and sometimes cheaper way of getting legislation enacted or repealed. In California, the process has long since moved from a tool of concerned citizens stymied by corrupt politicians to one employed by professional political operatives. Nowadays, gathering the huge number of signatures needed — 365,000 in 2016 for an initiative and 585,000 for a constitutional amendment — in a specified amount of time requires the assistance of professionals. That makes the process expensive and that again moves governance away from the people and into the hands of the BIGS.

For example, the $15 minimum wage was bludgeoned through the California legislature in early 2016 in three days. The bill was presented as a "pass it or else" proposition. If it were not approved by the legislature with no exceptions and no allowances for regional economic differences, a major public employee union had threatened to sponsor a ballot initiative to create the $15 minimum wage. As George Skelton, a columnist for the *Los Angeles Times*, explained it:

> *Labor wouldn't agree to [any] regional differences. It vowed to fight for a ballot initiative. That scared Democratic legislative leaders. It meant many millions of union dollars would be spent on a ballot measure — rather than on Democratic candidates for the legislature. It also would make it harder to raise union money for another Democratic cause: An initiative to extend an expiring "soak the rich" tax . . . for schools.*

The *Los Angeles Times* headlined that George Skelton column with its own sycophantic tribute — "The do-something Legislature outshines a do-nothing Congress." The *Times* also published photos of legislators hugging each other on the chamber floor. Were they pleased about giving low-wage Californians a boost in their income or for themselves for having preserved a major source of funding for their future political campaigns? We couldn't tell. We were also hard put to see what the members of the *legislature* had actually contributed to the bill to justify the nearly $200,000 annual compensation package they receive. From our vantage point, they hadn't contributed anything. That had all been worked out before the bill reached the Assembly floor by lobbyists for the union.[†]

The initiative process has proven so attractive that many groups submit issues for the ballot without any hope of qualifying them for a vote. With hundreds of thousands of signatures required costing as much as $5 a pop, few groups can afford the $2 million or so required to qualify an initiative *before* a campaign seeking voter approval can begin. Smaller groups seem to be in it for the free publicity they gain from the Secretary of State's announcements, to have their point of view promoted on a neutral website, and to demonstrate to the governor and the legislature that they are serious players and their issue is a serious public policy matter.

Because Republicans tend to vote more consistently than Democrats — and especially in pri-

---

[†]Taking credit where it isn't deserved extends to campaigns as well. One mailing piece we saw for a first term member of the California Assembly running for reelection in 2016 was sponsored by JobsPAC. It turns out to be a self-proclaimed bipartisan coalition of California employers who hide behind such names as Govern for California Action Committee, the Spirit of Democracy California, and Parents and Teachers for Putting Students First. In short, no one has a clue who may be funding this PAC. It does include major firms in BIG tobacco, BIG energy and BIG accounting. JobsPAC said this candidate "streamlined business regulations, balanced the state budget, kept property taxes under control . . ." and more. He apparently did this by himself without any help from the governor or the 129 other members of the legislature. Please. Do the people running JobsPAC think voters are that naïve or is the mailer really intended as an ego boost for the candidate to guarantee support for matters of interest to JobsPAC members but not yet identified?

mary elections — issues that tended to be blue in nature found their way onto the June ballot where Republicans could muster sufficient votes in a red state to get many of them approved. As a result, the Democrats voted to place citizen initiatives and most big bond issues on the November ballot exclusively when their voters were more likely to show up at the polls.

The Democrats did allow one exception: If the *legislature* — which they have controlled almost every year since 1970 — wants a constitutional amendment, bond issue or some other matter to be decided by the voters, that issue can be settled in a primary election.

Despite all the changes, the initiative process still seemed out of control. To hold down the number of issues that the voters might face on any given election day, California now allows the legislature to adopt an initiative into law *before* it gets to a public vote. If the "catch-up" law is signed by the governor, the need to fight a ballot issue campaign is obviated. That is what happened with the $15 minimum wage issue.

The liberal BIGs are so confidant that they can dictate agenda and policies that they decided to make the *Citizens United* decision an issue on the November 2016 ballot. Despite a potentially long ballot that will test the patience of even the most dedicated citizen, the legislature and a few big lobbying groups have decided to ask voters — for the first time — for an *opinion* on whether California should do everything in its power to rescind the decision. Although many oppose making elections into the equivalent of a public opinion poll, this important element of direct democracy seems destined to do exactly that.

With mandatory voting, discussed above, and an active group of Voter Issue Alliances, discussed below, the unions might not have been able to get the $15 minimum wage passed in the legislature. But since it did, it demonstrates how dominant lobbycratic governance has become in parts of the United States.

VOTER ISSUE ALLIANCES

With a lot of money on hand, certain voter groups can be targeted to produce the results that people behind the money desire. Nothing like the legitimacy of a government chosen by the people to accomplish ends of benefit to those with money

To combat the power of money in politics, a new force in government has been created called Voter Issue Alliances — or VIAs. VIAs recognize that citizens are concerned with and have opinions on many issues, but feel deeply about one or two issues on the political agenda. VIAs form around a single issue, are organized exclusively on the Internet, and aim their message at candidates for office to extract a pledge on how they will react to that issue when in office. With nurturing, VIAs can become as powerful and as influential as any political action committee or super PAC. They can be the public support for a Congressional caucus, giving strength to its members.

After all, the big money PACs and superPACs are generally formed by rich individuals, organizations or companies with similar broad economic and philosophical interests. As a result, the leaders of PACs have the freedom to pick and choose candidates and spend unaccountable money on their behalf to further the issue or issues that most concern them. It makes for a particularly potent political class where elected officials, senior technocrats and Washington-based lobbying executives feed off of each others' power bases. That is what lobbycratic governance produces.

Voter Issue Alliances do the same thing — not representing an economic interest or concern, but arguing for a particular position on a single issue on behalf of individual voters. Participants in a VIA will need to know only when the issue is in play in the political arena and which candidates or elected officials to notify of their potential support or opposition at a forthcoming election. Because of their relative simplicity, VIAs have the potential of replacing money with actual countable *votes*.

Money in politics, after all, is designed to influence voting for a particular flavor. If voting were locked up because voters had made up their minds about a single overriding issue of importance before the money could be effectively spent — the political landscape could be recast.

Here's how VIAs work in practice:

- All VIAs are formed around a single political issue. People are encouraged to participate in a VIA if the issue in question has overriding importance to them economically, socially, culturally or intellectually. It is anticipated that some politically active individuals could participate in a few VIAs, so long as the various issues are not in conflict. They could favor a strong position on Israel and a comprehensive approach to health matters. Like PACs, VIAs could eventually come to exist at every point along the left to right political continuum.

- The competition for support among VIAs will not be in terms of the money they can raise but on the actual votes they can deliver to a candidate for public office. Unlike PACs, which waste more than half the money they raise by promoting candidates and issues with television ads and direct mailing pieces aimed at or going to the 50-+ percent of Americans who do not vote, VIAs will concentrate on the 15 percent or so politically active and concerned citizens who have the ability to influence the rest of the population that votes.

- How do VIAs actually work? They employ a single formal weapon to fight their political battles. It is called a **statement of commitment**. A statement of commitment frames an issue and the favored position on that issue in simple and clear terms. VIA participants are then asked to sign a pledge to vote only for candidates that come closest to supporting the position in the Statement of Commitment.

- The role of the paid VIA managers is to elicit unequivocal statements from political candidates on the issue and then bring this information to the attention of VIA participants and the general public. As an election approaches, the VIA reminds its participants of its statement of commitment and the names of the candidates who have pledged their support for the commitment.

- The key to making the VIA effective is the Internet. Through an active email or social media connection between the VIA manager and VIA participants—and with new word of mouth techniques for the participants to use — the VIA becomes a powerful political force. Voting is no longer casual or viewed as a painful duty, but becomes recognized as the best pro-active means of changing the way society deals with specific issues.[†]

The VIA concept offers a different way to achieve what a PAC seeks to gain. The principal difference is that PACs were invented by lawyers seeking ways around election finance laws. The VIAs, on the other hand, were developed by public policy consultants with experience in managing issues

---

[†]Move-on.org offers an alternate process. If "you see something that needs a change . . . start a petition on MoveOn's website. You recruit your friends to sign it, and they, in turn, share it with their friends. We send it out to some fellow MoveOn members, and they sign on too, so we send it to everyone in your city, your state, or maybe even all 8 million MoveOn members . . . You use our petition tools to ask them to call their representatives, get more signers, and go to events. You deliver it to the person who has the authority to make the change. Your campaign makes headlines, and the decision maker is forced to respond. All you need is a good enough idea and the willingness to put in the time." But does it actually work?

and developing support when financial resources were not always readily available.

MONEY

Although Jesse Unruh, the speaker of the California Assembly between 1961 and 1969, once famously said that money is the mother's milk of politics, he knew better than most that money is only a means for harvesting *votes*. You spend money to get people to vote for your candidate or issue and often against someone else's candidate or issue.

Money has come to dominate elections as fewer and fewer people participate in the process. Look at some of the statistics of what was spent during the 2016 Presidential primaries:

- Republican Presidential candidate Donald Trump spent $3.7 million to win the New Hampshire primary. By contrast Governor Jeb Bush spent 10 times as much and finished fourth with one-third as many votes.

- The high cost of U.S. elections is probably better appreciated in per vote terms: The Trump camp spent about $37 for each vote received while the Bush campaign consumed more than $1,000 per vote. If those numbers don't appall you, then books like this won't likely move you to do anything anyway.

The main source of the big money used in national and local campaigns has come from rich individuals and big organizations free to spend as much as they like. The key aspect of the right to unlimited spending is that it must be *independent* of the candidate or cause. So when a Los Angeles city councilman says he has nothing to do with paying for billboards promoting his campaign for office — yet makes the rules for the city with regard to regulating billboards — should we really think that the billboard company is donating the space because it believes in good government?

Citizens United has also opened the door to major foreign involvement in U.S. elections through the purchase of shares of public corporations. Ellen Weintraub, a member of the Federal Election Commission, writing in *The New York Times* in 2016 suggested this as one of the unintended consequences of *Citizens United.* As matters now stand, any foreign group with an interest in the outcome of U.S. elections could create a U.S. corporation, load it with cash, and then direct its assets be given to a protected 501(c)(4) organization supporting a favored candidate. It may be happening now. Only the foreign groups and their lawyers would know if they are and neither are likely to reveal anything.

Weintraub suggested that corporations with more than 20 percent of its shares owned by foreigners should be prohibited from participating financially in any U.S. election through any source. Others note that *Citizens United* is flawed because it allows corporate leaders to spend shareholder money to further their personal political beliefs; those beliefs may be contrary to the beliefs of many of their shareholders. Another person was shocked when he realized that any group of individuals could form a corporation to provide unlimited funds on behalf of a candidate or cause even though individually the members of that group would be strictly limited in how much they could give to a campaign. That kind of work-around seems to violate America's basic belief in one person, one vote.

LOBBYING

Something needs to be done to interrupt the revolving door that allows technocrats to move back and forth between private enterprise and government agencies. Because of the revolving door, policy control by lobbying organizations is enhanced while the individual improves his or her influence and earning power. I think the country needs to debate some of the following restrictions on technocrats and lobbyists:

- Mandate that any move from a position of influence in a special interest organization to a policy position in the legislative or executive branches — or vice versa — would require an intervening stint of living a period of time at some distance from Washington, D.C. The feeling in the rest of the country is that those who live and work within the Beltway need to experience life close to how their fellow 324 million Americans experience it.

- An equally important step might be to prohibit any technocrat of a certain rank — say the equivalent of GS15 or higher — from working for a lobbying organization less than three years after the technocrat leaves government.

- In addition to, or in substitution for, the provision above, any member of a Congressional staff or executive branch agency should be required to recuse him or herself from any involvement in a contract award to an industry with which the individual has had a lobbying connection within the previous three years.

MENS REA RULE

Part of ending the power of lobbycratic governance requires signalling that major changes are coming to the legal system as well as to voting procedures. Take the *mens rea* rule involving criminal intent. Representative Jim Sensenbrenner, a Republican from Wisconsin and a member of the House Judiciary Committee, advocates a principle of law that is often forgotten but stoutly opposed by the judicial bureaucracies. A *mens rea* rule requires the state to not only prove that (1) a person committed a crime *but (2)* that the person knew that the act was against the law.

Today, penalties for most criminal offenses are imposed for committing an illegal act; the laws do not require that the individual knew he — or she — was doing something wrong. Teresa Giudice, the star of *The Real Housewives of New Jersey* and an author, spent most of 2015 in federal prison for engaging in a fraud having to do with filing for bankruptcy while hiding income and assets she owned. She claimed at trial and under oath not to have known about her husband's financial dealings and that she merely signed documents he put in front of her. He began his 41-month sentence for the same crime in March 2016.

Sensenbrenner's Criminal Code Improvement Act would require the government to prove a crime had been committed and that a person *intended* to violate a criminal statute by his or her conduct, conduct that a reasonable person would deem wrong. The Obama administration opposes *mens rea* as a Republican attempt to protect corporations and white-collar criminals from prosecution.

Sensenbrenner responded to the White House opposition in a February 2016 column in *The Wall Street Journal.* He noted that corporations are likely to have legal departments to guide them on what is lawful or not; rich individuals also have their own lawyers to provide advice. Little guys have neither. Sensenbrenner adds that "the real motive in opposing the *mens rea* law is to protect the Justice Department, which wants to preserve its ability to secure easy convictions."

Is this divide real or a smoke screen? Without *mens rea* the Justice Department has much more ability to force a case to settlement, put another bad guy, away, claim to have protected another victim, and add a personal coonskin to the wall. It makes for good campaign literature when a district attorney or U.S. attorney seeks elected office, but it doesn't necessarily make for *justice.* Rather than dismiss *mens rea* rules as protecting those who don't need protection, these rules should be looked at as a way to improve our judicial system in terms of fairness.

IMPROVING THE LEGAL SYSTEM

To further improve the legal system, end the monopoly that provides lawyers with power, profit and protection. I would do this by appointing non-lawyers to all agencies and governing bodies that have anything to do with the administration of justice, the establishment of legal policy and the training and licensing of lawyers.

Secondly, I would re-establish the public's ownership of all aspects of the legal system by insisting that at least 10 percent of all appellate judges and members of judicial boards be non-lawyers. I would involve other professionals — such as clergy, notaries, consultants, negotiators, mediators and psychologists — in a broad range of matters arising in legal activities. Let's once again put the focus of the law on providing justice rather than serving those with the money to manipulate the system. Along these lines, let's prohibit the recent practice of deep pocket groups investing in bodily injury, wrongful death and libel cases in the hope of scoring big earnings to add to their profits, endowments and other income.

As we have pointed out elsewhere, the American legal system is nearly broken. Not only has it become unreasonably expensive, it is particularly cumbersome and frustrating in civil disputes. Resolving civil disputes in traditional ways should remain available to any potential litigant. But we also clearly need a fresh way to settle civil conflicts — promptly, inexpensively and conclusively.

One such new approach might be called a *legal auction*. It would be like a Dutch auction — a mechanism to establish the value of a business, piece of property or some other object. Dutch auctions work this way: Both sides set the price at which they would be willing to buy or sell the item in question. Since each person in a Dutch auction is willing and qualified to buy *or* sell an item at a price he or she sets, the highest buying price becomes the real value of the item to the participants. No room for phony negotiating tactics, false bids or other gimmicks to juice value.

In a civil legal auction in which a tangible object is in dispute, both sides would be forced to state the exact amount of money or precise conditions under which they would accept or give to the other side to end a dispute. I propose empowering a new judicial office called a *legal referee* to determine the legitimacy of each party's claim by requiring everyone involved to swear, under penalty of perjury, to the truthfulness of every aspect of their participation in the new proceeding. The idea would be to squeeze out the puffery, posturing and phony demands that are now so much a part of the negotiating positions in the current legal process.

In other disputes, where a tangible object is not involved, legal auctions could be similar to the procedure now in place for settling Internet domain disputes. In this case, a legal referee would consider the claims of each side as well as all agreements in place, ask either party questions pertinent to an understanding and clarification of the dispute, refer any elements of the case to independent experts for their examination and opinion if necessary, and eventually present a *finding* — the referee's analysis of the issues, a statement of the differences between the parties and an opinion of the amount of money and conditions that would settle the matter fairly. Each party would then have several days to submit a sealed bid at or above the finding amount and the acceptable conditions to end the dispute. Would this work? We think it could once the principals, lawyers, accountants and consultants all realize that truth and facts, rather than narrower individual interests and imaginary affronts, become paramount in the process.

WHERE DO WE GO FROM HERE?

Hopefully, some of the ideas advanced for ending lobbycratic governance will be worth discussing. To be sure those lobbyists, technocrats, lawyers and public officials who would be most affected by the suggestions in this chapter will be dismissive. They will say that there isn't any problem, that the Constitution's three branches are fully functioning as the Founding Fathers intended, and that *Citizens United* can be fixed in several ways to return us to the *status quo ante*. But denial might be an attempt to protect the status quo .

However, the problems presented, the examples given and the case studies discussed in this book give ample evidence that something needs to be done to guide the ship of state in a new direction, one that the vast majority of Americans can consistently support.

11.
CONCLUSION

This book has tried to show the impact of government changes over the past 50 years. During that time, governance has evolved from a mechanism that we were taught in schools to a system that operates quite differently. Put as simply as possible, government today allows technocrats, lobbyists and lawyers to effectively control how the rules determining what is and is not permitted by society are written, implemented and enforced.

This book has also suggested some ways that the mechanisms of government might be changed to once again put America on a path toward a government of, by and for the people. The trend, however, toward this goal has faltered in the wake of *Citizens United*. That ruling has ushered in the current era where money plays an oversized role in the way many governmental decisions are made.

It is common to read a polemical book such as this and dismiss the broad theme because the reader is aware of an exception or two to the evidence and examples offered. Of course, it is the right of every reader to decide the validity and applicability of any presentation. But these pages ought to be judged in terms of the *trends* suggested and the *patterns* identified, even if all the details don't comport with all aspects of every reader's observations, impressions and experience. My goal has been to capture people's attention with facts as they have come tumbling out of recent news cycles in the hope that they would be seen in the same general way as I have seen them.

While it is easy to date noticeable changes in how the U.S. government actually operates based on the *Citizens United* decision, that is probably too facile. The slow erosion of control from representatives of the people to technocrats seems to have been occurring from the days of the New Deal.

And its acceleration continues unabated to this day. The Americans with Disability Act is a good example of this. The 1990 law codified a sincere effort to be fair to World War II, Korean and Vietnam war veterans as well as kids with congenital diseases that left them unable to do what their friends could do. The ADA was intended to end the exclusion and segregation from public accommodations for those with physical challenges. People generally liked the idea in principle until government officials, advocates and lawyers began writing the regulations that made compliance costly, disruptive and intrusive of the interests of the vast majority of citizens. As always, the devil came in the details.

In the days before the New Deal, legislation such

as the 1930 Smoot-Hawley Tariff Act was written by Congress to encompass the details needed to determine the import duty to be paid on products coming into the United States. Later it was determined that all those details were too complex, too cumbersome and too burdensome to be determined by legislators alone. Congress soon figured out how to share some and delegate most of the work. Philip K. Howard, writing in *The Wall Street Journal,* didn't mince words. He called Congress —

> *a lazy institution that postures instead of performing its constitutional job.*

Preferring to consider general policy questions from afar rather than to get deep into the trivia trenches, Congress left details to civil servants. They were soon involved with advocates on every side of an issue. Regulations became the battleground. Once the ADA rules went into effect, the lawyers and their clients reacted negatively to the high costs of making the changes mandated.

Lawsuits ensued on both sides — for individuals as well as large groups forming a "class" of plaintiffs. Juries soon began making significant awards. More lawsuits were filed against miscreants and more rancor permeated American society railing against nanny government. Some argued that equality is about giving everyone an equal chance, not about giving everyone an equal result.

Here's just one example. I work in a small office building on the Westside of Los Angeles. The building has offices for about 30 businesses — lawyers, medical practitioners, architects, software developers, consultants, product distributors and the like. For the seven years we have been in the building, an electric water fountain had been located near the elevator on the second floor — a device that stood four feet tall. Then it was gone. I asked the building's owner what happened to this nice perk. He responded in an email:

> *The drinking fountain is not ADA accessible [because it was too high for people in wheel chairs] so had to go. I could get sued for that — but no requirement to provide any fountain.*

Here was another clear example of how our lives have been altered by the change in the way government operates. A landlord believes he can be held liable, under the Americans with Disability Act, for not having the *right* water fountain, but cannot be held accountable for having *no* water fountain. When 10 percent of the population determine how the other 90 percent live elements of their lives, you get the kind of atmosphere that has poisoned the politics of America. Some ask the same question concerning transgender bathroom rights. Why must the vast majority of Americans respect the preferences of a fraction of the population while the preferences of the vast majority can be ignored?

Another example. A municipal swimming pool in Brooklyn has been accommodating Hasidic Jewish women for years with hours when no men were permitted to use the facility. Then someone perceived a violation of the separation of church and state; the special hours were cancelled. Hasidic women get no exercise. But no worries, New York's Commission on Human Rights is on the case. Is there any wonder that so many Americans have become so angry at the way governmental rules have come to complicate their lives and happiness?

Listen to the words of one Tea Party activist:

> *People are sick and tired of the same old, same old — just money corrupting the political process. They work hard, they vote for elected officials, and they expect them to keep their promises.*

Another observer reached the same conclusion on the sameness of politics, but described it this way:

> *. . . the Republican Party is really just a wing of . . . the Demopublican Party — an oligarchy with two wings: the Democratic wing that sets the agenda and the Republican wing whose main function is to help implement that agenda . . . all members in both wings of the [single] party fully understand the importance of the theater aspect of the political game, never losing sight of the fact that their overarching, joint objective is to stay in power. Everything else about the game is secondary.*

Others echo the same phenomenon, but from other angles. Here's how *Los Angeles Times* columnist Steve Lopez captures the mood:

> *The message . . . is that there's a hunger for [the] nontraditional. Only those with an interest in the status quo would want more of the same that Hillary Clinton or some Republican establishment candidates represent.*

We see the ferment in the 2016 electoral campaign a little differently. We see a public that has lost control of its government, is frustrated by the situation and is searching for a means of regaining the control they thought they previously had. That has led to the very high expectation of what elected officials can do. This book questions that expectation.

I do not believe that elected officials are the root cause of the malaise the people of the United States are now feeling about their government. The malaise is caused by shifting alliances of lobbyists, technocrats and lawyers who are continually tinkering with the machinery of government to find solutions to problems that satisfies *their* philosophy, *their* interests and the interests of *their* clients.

While *elected officials* may offer comments during the process in which these alliances are working their magic, political power does not run *through* them any more. Political power now seems to move *around* elected officials to the technocrats. As a result, the anger that the American people feel toward elected officials is misdirected. That anger should not be aimed at high-ranking members of the Democratic or Republican parties — or the elite behind these two groups — but to the *organizations* that are controlling the process that determines how American governance now works.

Take the effort of Governor Brown of California to reform the state's Environmental Quality Act. It has been stopped by unions involved in the building trades in conjunction with the Natural Resources Defense Council. The unions help builders win variances and exceptions to restrictive laws at the local level in return for guaranteeing union jobs on their projects. To reform the law would rob the unions as well as the environmentalists of their juice. Result: The politicians prove helpless to change matters in the face of the organizational pressure; in the process, the people's interests are ignored.

The strength of the construction unions in this case is an interesting "exception that proves the rule." The big trade unions are no longer the powerful force in the economy they once were; their membership numbers are down sharply and strikes no longer have the impact they once had except in a few sectors. But as unions have grown weaker in the general economy, those representing government employees have gained enormous strength and power. As a result, they represent a significant influence in lobbycratic governance.

Another example of lobbycratic governance at work comes in the non-confirmation of Justice Merrick Garland to the Supreme Court. The Senate has refused to hold hearings in 2016 on the nominee, preferring to leave the choice of a successor to Justice Scalia to the new President. The philosophical tilt of a narrowly divided court is in the balance.

But what was really surprising was the declaration of Senate Majority Leader Mitch McConnell who said in an interview:

> I can't imagine that a Republican majority in the United States Senate would want to confirm, in a lame-duck session, a nominee opposed by the National Rifle Association.

Wow! No less an elected official than someone of Senator Mitch McConnell's rank stating as clearly as possible the control lobbycratic governance exercises today.[†] *The New York Times* noted editorially that even though 90 percent of Americans and three-quarters of the members of the NRA accept the need for universal background checks prior to someone being permitted to purchase a weapon, elected officials will not overrule an organization that opposes those proposed rules.

How did this happen? How does an elected official *not* exercise the power he is given by the electorate? There are lots of reasons, but one that stands out involves *timing*. It takes a while for an elected official to know enough about the complex structure and arcane rules of government — and the people who have written those rules — to deal effectively with them.

But about the time that an elected official has the kind of confidence required to make changes, term limits or new electoral opportunities get the office holder thinking about the other spheres that would increase his status and perhaps influence. As a result, typically the elected official moves on to deal with another set of technocrats but generally the same lobbyists. By this stage of a political

---

[†] At around the same time, the Humane Society of the United States said a compromise ivory control law in Vermont "would be worse than no law." With that, the bill was withdrawn and killed. Just like that! It is another example of how politicians defer to major organizations,which brook no compromise in pursuit of their objectives and make no contributions to those who waiver in their support.

career, the elected official recognizes the power of the lobbyists to work with the technocrats and fund a political campaign. He or she soon comes to accept the role we have described as that of a "concierge" — someone who may tinker at the policy fringes but essentially smooths the path to an end the lobbyists, technocrats and lawyers have agreed to while the elected official spends his or her time tending to constituent's needs.

If you are still doubtful, let me pose a question. What if someone had an idea that all bicycle traffic ought to *face* oncoming traffic as a way to reduce the rising number of car versus. bicycle accidents. How do politicians react to an idea like this today? Rather than drafting legislation and holding hearings, today's legislator first talks to traffic bureaucrats who in turn seek the views of bicycling advocates and safety groups. No one talks to the public. Doesn't that tell you how things have changed?

It doesn't always happen this way, of course, because exceptions to this neatly laid down pattern can always occur. But the exceptions just highlight a trend, just as the line splitting the peaks and valleys on a financial chart.

There is an American tendency to accept the precision of whatever research may underlie a political position. It seems to be something in America's DNA. Here's how *The Politics of Numbers* puts it:

> *America has become a nation of statistics watchers*
> *. . . an increased share of federal money is distrib-*
> *uted to states and localities according to various*

statistical formulae and criteria. The making of economic policy as well as private economic decisions hinges on fluctuations in key indicators.

Information gathering in America began with the first census conducted in Virginia in 1625. It was taken to refute rumors in London that the colony was dying out. Later a census was mandated in the Constitution — to determine how to apportion representation in the House of Representatives. James Madison argued that a population count ought to be expanded in order to aid legislation, calling it ". . . an opportunity of obtaining the most useful information . . . in order to know the various interests of the United States . . ."

In 1810 the government added a census of manufacturers; in 1840 information was collected regarding agriculture, schools, literacy and the mentally disabled. In 1850 it began to assemble data on libraries, crime and deaths. By 1880, the flood of statistics was praised as "the great picture of our social and physical freedom . . ."

The penchant for more and more numbers grew following World War II and the introduction of federal financing through monetary grants to the states. Urban renewal projects live and breathe on the basis of numbers concerning unemployment, crime, schools, vacancies and a lot more to prove a new need or bolster a renewal.

If anything, the fascination with numbers keeps growing. Technocrats feel comfortable proposing something if they have the support that a public opinion poll, a consultant's report or a scientist's study provides. No matter that most of the data may well be approximate or even inaccurate. A document, printed and bound, with a date, fancy logo and a few Ph.D. credentials sprinkled among the researchers, are wondrously mesmerizing. The lobbyists, of course, know this and happily pay to have this kind of "careful, thoughtful independent" research done whenever needed.

But are the people better off for this ruse? Probably not. Just as a love for numbers may be in America's DNA, so exactitude is an American obsession. Whether the measurement of a graduation rate or the calculations required for a trip to the moon, we want everything down to the last two decimal places.

> **But what if we took a quantum view of politics? If _trends_ and _tendencies_ were studied, we probably would move much faster and just as securely as waiting for yet another "definitive" report to give us a "clearer" picture of some target.**

So in thinking about what this book has offered, think more in terms of the general trends discussed rather than in the "proof" or "evidence" that locks down each point of view. There may not be as much of the latter as some readers would like, but certainly these pages have taken into account all the key current trends.

A final example that may prove of interest. Recently, we were invited to help a corporate client respond to a local government's sudden questioning of the company's right to operate a recycling center. The question arose despite the fact that the client has been in business at the same location for more than 30 years without a single complaint from the public or a government entity.

After some investigation, it appeared that an inspector had overlooked a permit in the file. All the subsequent questions and requests for documentation seemed to amount to a face-saving exercise to cover a bureaucratic error. But once one question was asked, more came. One of the subsequent issues posed by a deputy city attorney concerned whether the client's facility met current standards for noise limits. We said yes, but we also knew the only acceptable answer required carefully collected and documented data. So we engaged a scientist to take a series of audio measurements that demonstrated that the recycling machinery did not emit more sound than a common household washing machine. The *data* satisfied everyone.

The client, however, grumbled at the expense of the study when the result proved the expectation. I said that he exhibited the typical difference between the attitude of how a small business sees government and how big business deals with the same institution. The former for the most part, treat government as the enemy — something to be avoided because in their experience that they always want a pound of flesh that consumes either time or money.

Big business, on the other hand, sees government as a potential ally and avenue to do more business, done more consistently and at a greater profit. The client stopped in his tracks and asked how that is possible. I explained that in his case his recycling earnings are dependent on the vagaries of the economy — when there is strong demand for scrap, the price for recycled material goes up; when the economy turns soft, demand slows down.

Big companies can't avoid the same cycles, but they can protect themselves against the worst of the peaks and valleys. For example, if a government were to require all local businesses within its jurisdiction to use a given amount of locally available recycled material in their own manufacturing operations, the guaranteed trade would ameliorate the up and down nature of the business cycle. I asked the client what would happen to the price of scrap plastic and cans if everyone molding plastic packaging or rolling aluminum sheets were required to use some locally *recycled* material in their final products? Wouldn't the price steady and the market remain fairly stable? Absolutely, he said.

Isn't this what the farmers of Iowa did in asking the government to specify a percentage of ethanol in every gallon of gasoline sold to the American public? Isn't the lobbying organization formed by the ethanol producers a key to campaign funding for many elected officials in Iowa — including Presidential candidates? And what government official today is going to turn his back on being able to say that he has worked to end Middle Eastern control of our fuel supplies? Or endorse the benefits of recycling — save the earth for our grandchildren's grandchildren? The client got the point. It is both a lesson on how government works and how government has been used by the BIGS.

One more point along these lines. Henry Ford is often quoted as having said:

> *Any man who thinks he can be happy and prosperous by letting the government take care of him, better take a closer look at the American Indian."*

Fair point, but the list of government programs to support those below the poverty line are so numerous that it is said that some people can bring in as much as $60,000 a year by filling out a few forms once or twice a year — a sum far more than someone earning $15 an hour can earn by *working* eight hours a day, 40 hours a week. *The Detroit Free Press* has reported on women having multiple children because each brings an additional payment under the Aid to Dependent Children program.

But those who oppose these kinds of government programs or work up such a hatred for those who cheat the system should understand that the issue is not the substance of the programs themselves, but how these programs get created, approved, managed and funded year after year.

Remember, too, the roles that technocrats, lobbyists, lawyers and politicians now play. Only then can citizens begin the process of changing the dynamics of government that so bothers them.

12.
APPRECIATION/
BIBLIOGRAPHIC NOTES

No book of this size on a topic with so many possible angles to pursue is the work of one person alone. At the very least most of the observations have been made over a lifetime and most of the ideas discussed in emails, phone calls, meetings and letters. A number of ideas and examples used here have been contributed by friends and associates who have heard of the project and then found germane items to pass along. I have given more than a dozen lectures on the themes associated with lobbycratic governance over the years to different groups, and much of the feedback from those sessions have been incorporated into this narrative.

The point, I think, is that at this stage of my career

in public policy consulting, I don't know where every story originated, how an idea I read or heard may have refined my thinking, or who might be ultimately responsible for a point made or an example given.

I do know that a number of people have been involved in my life and work long before this project got underway. They have listened to my thoughts, given back with their own comments and suggested new approaches that I then explored. My penchant for clipping articles to share with others has triggered notes and ideas that have helped form the conclusions I reached in this book

The point is that what is reported in these pages developed long before I saw a strong enough pattern to begin setting the ideas down in some kind of coherent fashion. As a result, I cannot identify just how much I have relied on the wisdom and contribution of friends and colleagues for what I express here. The acknowledgement list below surely misses some and is in alphabetical order to avoid trying to rate the value of the help I received.

William P. Butler	A longtime friend and colleague in public policy consulting work who has contributed a ton to my knowledge of how the government really works.
Maria Cucho	Maria is not only Assistant to the Publisher of The Americas Group, she is also originally Peruvian. She contributed original research and observations to the discussion on elections in the country of her birth.

Barbara DeKovner-Mayer	My wife of nearly 35 years who has given me room and an audience to create, refine, sharpen and record a lot of what is in this book and has provided her own greatly appreciated thoughts in return.
Art Detman	A professional editor and friend who reviews every word and every design feature of my books with patience and care to ensure that what is said is accurate, consistent, grammatically correct and above all else clear.
Michael Harris	My brother, attorney, office mate and most constant critic who minces no words in telling me when he thinks I am wrong.
Kenneth M. Katz	Another old friend and long-time political colleague with whom I have shared a lot of ideas and worked on a lot of projects.
Cara Meskar	A brilliant, quick and particularly meticulous researcher who came on the scene late in this project but whose contributions have added mightily to the final product. She is a pleasure to work with.
Stanley Rogers	A friend, my brother's law partner, another office mate and constant observer of the political scene who has heard me talk about themes reflected in this book and has provided questions and details to refine them.

NOTES

As readers will have noticed, any extended parenthetical comments in the book that seemed appropriate or enlightening to the main discussion — but were sufficiently tangential to divert the flow of the narrative — are embedded as bottom-of-the-page footnotes highlighted by a dagger mark: †. By the same token, some readers may have noticed that there are no formal *reference* footnotes despite a number of direct quotations and mentions of other material.

This is a different approach to one I have taken in previous books. In most of those, I differentiated between textual and reference footnotes at the back of the book with a ^ for the former and the first three words of the quotation for the latter. I explained early on in each book that I wanted to signal readers to the two different types of footnotes at the back of the book so that they would know when I was making a parenthetical comment and when I was identifying a source that might or might not be of immediate interest.

I had first proposed this approach when I was a graduate student. My thesis advisor in the UCLA doctoral program thought it was a battle I wouldn't win with the librarians and shouldn't fight; save the topic, he said, for a time when your work is important enough that you can insist on such things. I don't know if this book qualifies as "important enough" but I have sufficient influence with the editors (I engage them) and the publisher (it is my company) to be able to insist on this format. I still think it is a service to readers to avoid overburdening them with unnecessary interruptions.

But now, some 60 years after that conversation with my advisor, I have altered my views on footnotes once again. I now find that *reference* footnotes, given the near universal availability and ease of locating sources on the Internet, are almost superfluous. As a result, I have eliminated them in this work and have tried as much as possible to provide sufficient information in the text to guide the curious to find the quotation or the facts in the original source on the Internet.

This will, no doubt, bother some readers who like to see the source of every statement — much like professional fact checkers charged with protecting reputations, law review editors who seem to equate the number of footnotes to the value of an article, and students or other writers who want a shortcut for their own research. For the most part, however, I have found that reference footnotes are not often reviewed by the vast majority of readers who find them distracting and bothersome — whether at the foot of a page or at the back of a chapter.

In addition, I decided to eliminate reference footnotes because I cannot pinpoint the source for all the ideas or comments about governance made here. My first political job was at the age of 15 when I became the principal receptionist at the Beverly Hills, California, campaign headquarters of Dwight D. Eisenhower. I have been professionally involved in dozens of government programs and political campaigns in the U.S., the United Kingdom and Central America ever since that first political job in 1952.

In addition, my work as a public policy consultant for nearly 50 years has involved me in countless projects that have colored my attitudes and refined my understanding of how government actually works. The engagements that have had particular influence included those undertaken for:

The American Revolution Bicentennial Commission
Jeffrey Barke for Board of Education (two campaigns)
Best Plans
Beverly Hills International Music Festival
Coalition of High School Alumni Organizations
Daon Corporation
The Da Vinci Exhibit
Department of Commerce
Department of Housing and Urban Development
Department of State
Destination Marketing
Foreign Policy Association of Panama
Friends Assisting Friends
Government of Panama
Government of St. Kitts-Nevis
High School America
International Publishers Alliance
Ivory Education Institute
London Chamber of Commerce & Industry

Pulsatron Technology Corporation
Sheet Metal Workers' International Association
South Coast Air Quality Management District
Tower Mortgage
Voter Issue Alliances

In some cases, the consulting assignments have spawned books, articles and published letters that offer insights into my thinking on topics that this book covers. As noted before, I am not entirely sure how what I think now on a multitude of topics came to me or has been refined over time.

A lot of that thinking has been captured in whole books I have written or co-authored, or included in chapters or sections involving political themes. These are listed below. Unless otherwise noted, they have been published by The Americas Group.

Betrayal in Panama, 2016 (Updated. Originally, *The Panama Problem*, 1993) [with Giullermo de St Malo A,]
The Essential Commemoration Management Guide, 2015 [with WilLiam P. Butler]
European Union Almanac, 1996 [with Adelheid Hasenknopf and Hans. J. Gross]
Just Sayin', 2016
Invasion, 1990
Ivory's Cultural Importance, Ivory Education Institute, 2012
Corruption, 2005
What a Great Idea, 2005
Panamanian Perspective, Foreign Policy Association of Panama, 1993
Panama's Position, Foreign Policy Association of Panama, 1972
The Quest for Foreign Affairs Officers, Carnegie Endowment, 1966 [with Frances Fielder]

I have contributed many major articles and letters to various publications on political themes over the years. Some of the comments or recommendations made in these contributions have found their way into this book. They are listed here in alphabetical order.

"A High Price," *The Washington Monthly,* September 1997
"Air Controllers," *Los Angeles Times*. November 23, 1981
"America and the Northern Marianas," *Los Angeles Times*, July 21, 1974.

"America's High Schools," *Yankee Bugle*, May 2012

"Banking by Lottery in Saigon is an Idea Worth Examining," November 10, 1973.

"Biggest Tax Swindle of Them All," *Los Angeles Times*, April 18, 1980.

"Boards of Directors," *Business Week*, June 19, 1971

"British Mail Service," *Santa Monica Evening Outlook,* September 29, 1978

"Coliseum Games," *Los Angeles Times*, March 28, 2012.

"Cowardice," *Los Angeles Times*. August 19, 1982.

"Foreign Aid's Uses Got Twisted in Panama," *The New York Times*, June 18, 1995

"Gov. Williams," *Los Angeles Times*, February 10, 1988

"How to Save Elephants and the Ivory Trade," *Los Angeles Times*, July 22, 2014.

"It's a Gas," *SMART Journal*, November 2013

"It's Too Important to Guess," *Los Angeles Times*, September 27, 1978

"The Los Angeles Primary Elections of 2015," *Yankee Bugle*, Summer 2015

"Making a Case to End Lawyers' Stranglehold on Legal System," *Los Angeles Business Journal*, July 28, 2008

"Memories of Wally Sterling," *Los Angeles Times*, July 20, 1985

"On Bureaucracy," *Newsbeat*, March 1983.

"On the Board," *Los Angeles Times*, August 18, 2004

"Panama Lottery Guarantees Win," *Miami Herald*, March 28, 1973

"Product Pricing," *Santa Monica Evening Outlook*, January 11, 1980.

"Settlements," *The Los Angeles Times*, August 24, 1981

"Some Answers—Posthaste," *The Los Angeles Times*, October 11, 1981

"Stereotyping Columbus" —*Liberty*, November/December, 1981.

"The Wrong Way to Save Elephants," *The New York Times*, [With Daniel Stiles] March 27, 2014

"Tilting at Windmills," *The Washington Monthly*, April 1990.

Finally, I have read a lot of books over the years that have informed my thinking and refined my ideas. They are still part of my personal library. It would be remiss not to mention some of those that I consider the most important in terms of themes and topics covered in this book:

Baker, James A., III, *The Politics of Diplomacy,* G. P. Putnam's Sons, 1995

Berg, A. Scott, *Wilson,* Simon and Schuster, 2013

Bordewich, Fergus M., *The First Congress,* Simon and Schuster, 2016

Califano, Joseph, *The Triumph and Tragedy of Lyndon Johnson,* Simon and Schuster, 2014

Clinton, Bill, *My Life,* Alfred A. Knoff, 2004

Dowd, Marureen, *Bushworld,* G. P. Putnam's Sons, 2004

Drew, Elizabeth, *Election Journal,* William Morrow & Co., 1989

Gans, Herbert J., *Deciding What's News,* Pantheon Books, 1979

Hersch, Seymour M., *Price of Power,* Summit Books, 1983

Leibovich, Mark, *This Town,* Blue Rider Press, 2013

Kaiser, Robert G., *Act of Congress,* Vintage Press, 2014

Kendall, Joshua, *First Dads,* Audible Books, 2016

Kurlansky, Mark, *Paper,* Audible Books, 2016

Mathews, Chris, *Tip and the Gipper,* Simon and Schuster, 2015

Mayer, Jane, *Dark Money,* Doubleday, 2016

McCullough, David, *Truman,* Simon and Schuster, 1992

Meacham, Jon, *Destiny and Power,* Random House, 2015

Panetta, Leon, *Worthy Fights,* Penguin Audio, 2014

Smith, Hendrick, *The Power Game,* Random House, 1988

Schlesinger, Arthur, Jr., *A Thousand Days,* Houghton Mifflin, 1965

Sorensen, Ted, *Kennedy,* Harper & Row, 1965

Stephanopoulos, George, *All Too Human,* Little Brown, 1999

Stockman, David, *Triumph of Politics,* Harper & Row, 1986

Toobin, Jeffrey, *A Vast Conspiracy,* Random House, 1999

Whatever the origins of what I have written in this book, I only hope that I have expressed them accurately here and that they make sense to readers. If readers are then encouraged to discuss the ideas with others and to try to make changes that put governance of the United States back on a path leading to an institution that functions of, by and for the people, the time and effort to prepare this book will have served a worthy purpose.

London Chamber of Commerce & Industry

Pulsatron Technology Corporation

Sheet Metal Workers' International Association

South Coast Air Quality Management District

Tower Mortgage

Voter Issue Alliances

OTHER BOOKS BY THE AUTHOR

Betrayal in Panama [2016] (with Guillermo de St. Malo A.)
  Reprint of *The Panamanian Problem* (with "Update" by GH)
Just Sayin' [2015]
The Essential Commemoration Management Guide [2015] (with William P.
  Butler)
The Essential Collection Management Kit [2014]
Ivory's Cultural Importance [2014]
The Essential Obamacare Checklist [2014]
Donation Dialog [2013]
Goat Cheese Guide (with Robert G. Gallagher) [2013]
Word of Mouth Advertising in the Real World [2013]
The Charity Event Planning Guide (with David Mirisch) [2013]
The Essential Event Planning Kit—1st, 2nd, 3rd, 4th, 5th, 6th, 7th, 8th,
  9th, 10th & 11th Editions [2001-2013]
European Union Almanac—1st & 2nd Editions (with Hans J. Groll
  and Adelheid Hasenknopf) [2006 & 2010]
Concentration—1st & 2nd Editions (with Kennith L Harris)
  [2006-2010]
Courting Failure (with Kennith L Harris) [2008]
  Introduction to Spanish edition [2014]
The Legacy of Leonardo da Vinci [2006]
Timeline—The Principal Events During the Lifetime of Leonardo da Vinci
  [2006]
Exhibit Catalog of the Da Vinci Experience —1st, 2nd, 3rd, 4th & 5th
  Editions [2006-2010]
Leonardo Quotebook [2006]
The Life and Contributions of Leonardo da Vinci (with Thomas
  Mankowski) [2006]
Coloring with Leonardo (with Daniel Mankowski) [2006]
The Essential Moving Planning Kit—1st, 2nd & 3rd Editions
  (with Mike H. Sarbakhsh) [2006-2010]
Promoting International Tourism—1st & 2nd Editions (with
  Kenneth M. Katz)
What a Great Idea! [2005]
The Definitive Southern California Diet (with Jeffrey I. Barke, M.D.)
  [2005]
The Hottest Ideas in Word of Mouth Advertising [2005]

The Complete Business Guide [2005]
The Essential Gift Planning Kit [2005]
The Essential Diet Planning Kit (with Jeffrey I. Barke, M.D.) [2005]
The Essential Wedding Planning Kit [2005]
The Essential Cooking Planning Kit [2005]
The Essential Project Planning Kit [2005]
Civility [2005]
Corruption [2005]
Grandparenting [2003]
The Essential Travel Planning Kit—1st & 2nd Editions [2006 & 2010]
Watch It! [2003]
Let Your Fingers Do the Talking [2003]
Talk Is Easy [2003]
The Ultimate Black Book—3rd Edition (with Kennith L Harris and Mark B Harris) [1999]
Don't Take Our Word for It! [1999]
How to Generate Word of Mouth Advertising (with Gregrey J Harris) [1999]
The Panamanian Problem (with Guillermo de St. Malo A.) [1993]
    Introduction to Spanish edition [2012]
Mapping Russia and Its Neighbors (with Sergei A. Diyakonov) [1993]
Power Buying (with Gregrey J Harris) [1993]
Talk Is Cheap (with Gregrey J Harris) [1993]
The Fascination of Ivory [1993]
The Ultimate Black Book—2nd Edition (with Kennith L Harris) [1993]
The Ultimate Black Book [1993]
The Panamanian Perspective [1993]
Invasion (with David S. Behar) [1989]
Commercial Translations (with Charles Sonabend) [1989]
From Trash to Treasure (with Barbara DeKovner-Mayer) [1983]
Panama's Position [1976]
The Quest for Foreign Affairs Officers (with Francis Fielder) [1963]
The History of Sandy Hook, New Jersey [1960]
Outline of Social Sciences [1958]
Outline of Western Civilization [1957]

INDEX

LOBBYCRATIC GOVERNANCE